MW00941405

Keeping You & Your Kids Sexually Pure

A How-To Guide for Parents, Pastors, Youth Workers, and Teachers

Also by La Verne Tolbert

Teaching Like Jesus: A Practical Guide to Christian Education in Your Church (Zondervan)

KEEPING You & YOUR KIDS SEXUALLY PURE

A How-To Guide for Parents,

Pastors, Youth Workers, and Teachers

La Verne Tolbert, Ph.D.

Copyright © 2007 by La Verne Tolbert, Ph.D.

ISBN: Hardcover   978-1-4415-1415-8
                Softcover   978-1-4415-1414-1

All rights reserved. No part of this publication may be reproduced, stored in
a retrieval system, or transmitted in any form or by any means—electronic,
mechanical, photocopy, recording, or any other—except for brief quotations in
printed reviews, without the prior permission of the publisher.

All Scripture quotations, unless otherwise noted, are taken from the *HOLY
BIBLE: NEW INTERNATIONAL VERSION*®. NIV®. Copyright © 1973, 1978,
1984 by International Bible Society. Used by permission of Zondervan. All rights
reserved. Scripture quotations marked AMPLIFIED are from the Amplified ®
New Testament. Copyright © 1954, 1958, 1987 by the Lockman Foundation.
Used by permission.

Scripture quotations marked KJV are from the King James Version of the Bible.

Scripture quotations marked NASB are from the NEW AMERICAN
STANDARD BIBLE ®. Copyright © The Lockman Foundation 1960, 1962, 1963,
1968, 1971, 1972, 1973, 1975, 1977, 1995. Used by permission.

Scripture quotations marked NKJV are from the New King James Version.
Copyright © 1979, 1980, 1982 by Thomas Nelson, Inc. Used by permission.
All rights reserved.

This book was printed in the United States of America.

To order additional copies of this book, contact:
Xlibris Corporation
1-888-795-4274
www.Xlibris.com
Orders@Xlibris.com
36972

CONTENTS

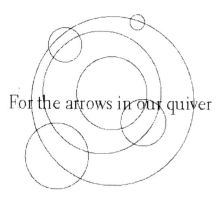

For the arrows in our quiver

acknowledgments

Years in the field and years of research are combined in this book. Along the way, many have encouraged, educated, and inspired me, notably Dr. Stan Weed, who mentored me throughout the dissertation process; Dr. Michael Anthony, who insisted I find the answer to a simple question; Pat Ware, who suggested the topic for my research; and Lakita Garth who introduced us.

For an environment at Talbot School of Theology that embraced my study even though it may have been a bit outside of the norm, I extend a special thank you to Dr. Dennis Dirks, dean, and Dr. Klaus Issler, then chair of the doctoral program. For her encouragement throughout the dissertation process, a special thank you to my friend Dr. Shelly Cunningham. For assistance with finding the impossible, thank you to Gracie Hsu of the Family Research Council; Biola librarian Bob Krauss; and Cheryl Stabler of the *Los Angeles Times*. For the research grant, thank you to the North American Professors of Christian Education. Finally, thank you, Dr. Sherwood Lingenfelter, for ushering me into the doctoral program in the first place.

To those who read this book in various drafts, thank you for your critique and suggestions: Dr. Minnie Claiborne, my prayer partner who entreats heaven daily on my behalf; Dr. Angela Griffiths, for her insightful and invaluable editorial comments; Paulette Bowman, Alesia Brown, Ed Cunningham, Shawnee Fisher, Jerry Gramckow, Dr. Stella Ma, Sonja Schappert, and Forrest Turpin. To those who lent their personal stories whether named, pseudonymous, or anonymous, thank you for your honesty and vulnerability.

This book was originally published by Zondervan, and it is with special regard that I thank my former editor, Jim Ruark, for his courage in accepting this work and for his superb attention to editorial detail that polished a rock into a smooth stone. Thank you!

To Irving, my husband, lover, and friend, for being as excited as I am about the next project and actually believing that it can be done, please know that it can't be done without you. Thank you for being the love of my life. Finally, to La Nej, thank you for your laughter, love, and obedience to our Lord. I'm so grateful for the gift that God gave me when he gave me you. Kiss, kiss, hug tight, never let go!

part 1

parents: the message begins at home

*Love the Lord your God with all your heart and with all
your soul and with all your strength. These commandments that I give you today are to be upon your hearts.
Impress them on your children. Talk about them when
you sit at home and when you walk along the road, when
you lie down and when you get up.*

Deuteronomy 6:5–7

The chubby twelve-year-old standing in the middle
of the room was demanding my attention. I had
picked her up from school, served her a snack, and
feeling my duties adequately met, gone back to writing at the computer. Obviously, having a child
around was quite new to me.

"Stop working. I'm home now!" she demanded.
I jerked around, a bit stunned at how clearly La Nej
articulated her need and at a loss for any words that
might couch a legitimate excuse for me to ignore it.
I thought of giving her a chore, of sending her to do
homework, or of assigning her the ever necessary
task of cleaning her room. But nothing came out of
my mouth, for within me a deeper request res-
onated. My heart heard her unspoken words, "I need
time with you."

Loving God and applying the principles of God's
Word gives parents a head start in raising their children. Impressing godly principles upon our children
is accomplished through the sacrificial gift of time.
Once we're *with* our children, teaching them God's
commandments is simple: We talk with them while
we're sitting, walking, lying down, and getting up.

chapter 1

great expectations

Lift up a standard for the people.
Isaiah 62:10 KJV

My daughter had two choices: Either she was going down the aisle a virgin or she was going down the aisle in a coffin.

This, of course, is hyperbole. Restated, it means that in our home the boundary lines for sexual purity were clear: Nothing less than virginity was acceptable.

* * *

I looked into the eyes of this child whom God had given me to raise, my twin sister's daughter. When she was born, I suggested naming her La Nej, which loosely means "snow" and for me was symbolic of a fresh, new beginning.

Eleven years later La Nej was in a foster home on Long Island, New York. Through prayers, letters, and urgent calls to the Department of Social Services, I was able to assume custody and flew three thousand miles to get my niece. I would later marry, adopt her, and raise her as my own daughter.

When I drove to the facility in upstate New York, the Holy Spirit was my navigator. I had no idea where I was heading, but I was determined to get there. The paperwork that would grant me custody was not yet final, but La Nej was permitted to come to Los Angeles on an "extended vacation."

The child was distraught when I arrived at the foster care facility. I later learned that her foster mother had taunted her, saying I wouldn't come for her after all. The quiet panic in her eyes turned to relief when she, standing outdoors despite the wintry weather, finally saw me walking toward her. "Kiss, kiss! Hug tight! Never let go!" she said as she wrapped her little arms tightly around my neck. It was a phrase I would hear often, one that would become a precious signature of the commitment we had made to each other.

We gathered La Nej's things, most of which I soon discarded. Her thick hair was braided in ugly little pigtails, and the striped woolen cap scrunched on her head looked third-hand. Since this was the day before her twelfth birthday, we had a wonderful excuse for a little pampering. I drove right to my favorite beauty salon in Manhattan and marveled at how different La Nej looked after a simple shampoo and set. Then we shopped till we dropped.

The world of beauty had been my career for more than ten years. A former magazine beauty and health editor, I had written two beauty books and in the process had relocated to Los Angeles, where I continued to write, travel, and consult. How would I juggle these responsibilities now that I was a single parent? I decided to think about it one day at a time, a lesson I had come to learn in my daily walk with God.

On the plane back to Los Angeles, the relief of finally getting La Nej out of the system gave way to the reality of my new responsibility. I realized that I had no idea how to raise a child. I thought about my own childhood and the emotional scars that had remained hidden for years, scars that resulted from being displaced from my parents at times, living with grandparents off and on, and occasionally in foster homes too. Perhaps I saw myself in La Nej. All I know is that I wanted her to make different choices than the ones I had made—poor decisions that resulted from raggedy self-esteem.

We sat down for our first serious talk immediately after breakfast while we were still in our bathrobes. Her eyes tried unsuccessfully to hide her surprise as I pulled out larger than life charts of the male and female reproductive organs, visuals I had used in public school classrooms during my volunteer years as a board member with Planned Parenthood.

"These are the ovaries. The egg comes from here once a month," I said as I made a fist and placed it below my stomach. The lecture continued as I charted the course of what happens when the sperm meets the egg. "The best way to keep the sperm from meeting the egg is to say no," I concluded.

Although I'm uncertain of how much she actually understood at that time, of this I am certain: La Nej knew that keeping herself sexually pure was of the utmost value. Later she would hear her options for going down the aisle repeated again and again and again and again. . . .

I had lectured with the best intentions. When I put the charts away, however, I vowed never to use them again with my or anyone else's daughter. There had to be a better way.

* * *

Research demonstrates that when parents expect their children to be abstinent, they are more likely to abstain from sex. Studies also show that when boundary lines become fuzzy or mixed messages are conveyed, like handing out condoms while telling teens to just say no, kids are confused about what's right and wrong.

All across America Christian parents are setting standards and raising the bar high. Like the mother on the antismoking billboard who says to an acquaintance who is puffing away on a cigarette, "Not in *my* house!" mothers and fathers everywhere are taking a stand. Children are expected to obey biblical guidelines that affirm sexual intercourse for marriage only. Period.

Messages from the media coupled with courses in the classroom present our children with a smorgasbord of options, including non-marital sex, same-sex sex, group sex, Internet sex, and combinations thereof. Society urges us to teach our children to say no to drugs and alcohol but draws the line there. When it comes to their most precious possession—their bodies—our children are learning that they have the *right* to have sexual intercourse. And parents have the right to say, "Not in *my* house!"

Boundaries

Christian psychologists Drs. Henry Cloud and John Townsend teach that setting boundaries is necessary and positive.[1] Simply put, boundaries are essential because they keep good things in and bad things out.

God defined the boundary for sexual intercourse, and that boundary is marriage between a man and a woman. Parents assume that their children understand this, but the vagueness that results from too little time together opens a Pandora's box subject to each child's individual interpretation.

One student said in a recent *Time* magazine article, "Parents haven't set boundaries, but they are expecting them." Children who want to discuss sexual ethics with their parents "can't get their attention long enough."[2] Investing time to build relationships with our children cultivates healthy talking ground. Here is where boundaries are set, and parents who do so realize that children feel safer and more protected with adults who are not afraid to be proactive.

* * *

Our daughter's friend Wendi was dressing for the prom with our daughter at our home. Wendi's dad had given her permission to spend prom night at the hotel where some of her other classmates were attending the after-party. When my husband learned that she planned to go to the hotel with her date after the prom, he confronted her.

"Since you're getting dressed in our home, you are expected to return here. I don't care what your father said. You may not spend the night at the hotel."

Wendi went home. An hour later she was knocking at our door, and when I opened it, she was standing there with a stack of clothes in her arms. "I'm moving in," she announced. And she did. She knew that we really cared about her and started calling me, "Mom," and Irving, "Dad." She followed our rules and stayed the entire summer before going to college.

* * *

The goal of Christian parents is to foster a home environment where children fall in love with God and obey him. Jesus said, "If you love me, you will obey what I command" (John 14:15). We teach our children that God's heart is broken when we disobey his commandments. God says:

> O that there were such an heart in them, that they would fear me, and keep all my commandments always, that it might be well with them, and with their children forever!
>
> Deuteronomy 5:29 KJV

God is not trying to keep us from having fun. He is protecting us. The standard of sexual purity is high because the cost of disobedience is so great. If we want our children to have a good life, we need to raise them up—above the garbage, above confusion and chaos, and up to God's standards.

When our children step outside the lines of safety, they fall prey to a host of unforeseen, unimaginable consequences. Forgiveness awaits the prodigal, but God does not wave a magic wand to erase the effects of sin. Nonmarital sexual intercourse is sin, and sin has its consequences. Shame, guilt, broken hearts, and shattered expectations are emotional scars that are immune to pills and ointments. And, no matter how much medicine is applied, many sexual diseases don't heal at all. According to the Centers for Disease Control and Prevention, approximately 65 million Americans are currently living with an incurable sexually transmitted disease (STD). Each year approximately 15 million people become infected with one or more STD. A whopping 25 percent of these infections occur in sexually active teenagers.[3]

The statistics for the deadliest STD, the human immunodeficiency virus/acquired immunodeficiency syndrome (HIV/AIDS), are even more alarming. Between 26 and 50 percent of those who contract the disease become infected in their teenage years or early twenties.[4] And this is the result of heterosexual, not homosexual, activity.

In other words, nearly *half* of all HIV infections occur in children who are living at home, wearing clothes that their parents bought, eating food that their parents prepared, sleeping in beds and living under roofs provided by their parents. Some have luxury items—cars—to drive to school. For many, conscientious mothers and fathers will work two or three jobs to pay thousands of dollars for four or five years of college tuition.

These sexually active children are too young to vote. If they had a toothache, they could not go to the dentist without their parents. Parents would be arrested if they intentionally neglected to provide food, clothing, or housing. And parents are responsible for maintaining insurance to pay for their children's medical care.

Where are these kids having sex? Sexually active teenagers admit that because they are in single-parent households or homes where both parents are working, they are left with many hours of unsupervised free time. Thus, they are having sex at home, sometimes in their parents' bed.

Bombarded by a social environment where sex is portrayed as essential to obtain friends and maintain popularity, where sex sells yet condoms are free, where violent, sexually explicit music assaults the psyche, where cable television and indecent commercials parade around the mental landscape of the youngest imagination, we need to stop and ask ourselves, "What on earth is happening?"

An objective analysis would surmise that children in contemporary society are victims of sexual exploitation. Desensitized and immature, kids view sexual intercourse as "no big deal." Parents should feel outraged that the children they struggle so hard to protect are constantly being violated.

With the emotional, psychological, and physical health of our children at stake, the time for feeling powerless is over. The wellbeing of our families and communities, and ultimately our country is on the line. Parents must take back the reins and declare to their children that sexual intercourse is for marriage only. This is not moralizing; nor is it preaching. It's *parenting*.

Sex Is God's Idea

We often forget that sex is God's idea. He designed it, and like everything else God created, sex is *good*. But God confined the sexual act to a specific union, and the sign over that door reads, "For husbands and wives only."

God protected humankind from the consequences of nonmarital sexual intercourse with the Old Testament law, "You shall not commit adultery" (Exod. 20:14). We see the benefits of fidelity to God through the example of Joseph, a handsome teenager who, when tempted, chose to run from sexual sin (Gen. 39:6-12). Because of Joseph's obedience, God used him to deliver his people, which illustrates that individual choices of morality ultimately affect the community and therefore have social ramifications that span well beyond the walls of the bedroom.[5]

Proverbs is replete with reminders that the proper context for sexual intercourse is within the marriage union.

> Drink water from your own cistern, running water from your own well. Should your springs overflow in the streets, your streams of water in the public squares? Let them be yours alone, never to be shared with strangers. May your fountain be blessed, and may you rejoice in the wife of your youth.
>
> Proverbs 5:15-18

The public disgrace of sexual immorality so vividly painted here by Solomon, King David's son, was sketched from the infidelity of his father, King David. The king was in the wrong place at the wrong time where he looked long at that which was not meant for his eyes. Filled with lust, he used his power and office to seduce another man's wife. When he learned afterward that his mistress was pregnant, his immediate response was to deny paternity. Failing in this, he resorted to the brutal murder of his lover's husband (2 Sam. 11-12).

For David's private sin, God meted out public humiliation in addition to telling David that the child would die.

This is what the LORD says:

> "Out of your own household I am going to bring calamity upon you. Before your very eyes I will take your wives and give them to one who is close to you, and he will lie with your wives in broad daylight. You did it in secret, but I will do this thing in broad day light before all Israel."
>
> 2 Samuel 12:11-12

David's favorite son, Absalom, in a failed attempt to overthrow the throne, had sexual intercourse with his father's concubines "on the roof . . . in the sight of all Israel" (2 Sam. 16:22). These consequences—the death of the child and David's public humiliation—may have been vivid in Solomon's mind as he wrote the proverbial caution.

The Israelites' idolatry, which involved sexual sin, resulted in their seventy-year captivity and the destruction of the holy city (Jer. 25:7-11). Scripture reports the depths of their degenerative behavior: "They have built the high places of Baal to burn their sons in the fire as offerings to Baal," an act so abominable that the omniscient Father says in utter disbelief that it had never even entered his mind (Jer. 19:5).

In the New Testament, amid the backdrop of an idolatrous and promiscuous culture, the apostle Paul constantly reminded Christians that violation of God's law was not without consequences. However the kingdom of God is defined—whether living presently in the authority and blessing of the King⁶ or in the future kingdom with the King—one fact is certain: Sexually immoral Christians are *not* included.

> Do you not know that the wicked will not inherit the kingdom of God? Do not be deceived: Neither the sexually immoral nor idolaters nor adulterers nor male prostitutes nor homosexual offenders nor thieves nor the greedy nor drunkards nor slanderers nor swindlers will inherit the kingdom of God.
>
> 1 Corinthians 6:9-10

Everyone who trusts in Jesus Christ as Savior and Lord has the power to live free from sexual sin. It's the exercise of that power—the same power that raised Jesus Christ from the dead—that makes the difference. The excuse that "everyone has needs" is not new. This same "It's my body and I'll do what I want to" philosophy was commonly offered by Christians in Paul's day. Paul explained to the Corinthian church that the body was not for sexual immorality, but for the Lord (1 Cor. 6:13-14).

Every time a Christian allows her body to be sexually touched by someone who is not her husband, Jesus Christ, like a rape victim, is violated against his will.

> Do you not know that your bodies are members of Christ himself? Shall I then take the members of Christ and unite them with a prostitute? Never! Do you not know that he who unites himself with a prostitute is one with her in body? For it is said, "The two will become one flesh." But he who unites himself with the Lord is one with him in spirit.
>
> 1 Corinthians 6:15-17

How are we to respond when faced with sexual temptation? We are to run for our lives! The Bible tells us to flee sexual immorality. The person who sins sexually is actually sinning against her own body (1 Cor. 6:18). Our bodies are not our own. We have been bought at a very, very high price paid by Jesus Christ himself.

> Do you not know that your body is a temple of the Holy Spirit, who is in you, whom you have received from God? You are not your own; you were bought at a price. Therefore honor God with your body.
> 1 Corinthians 6:19-20

With Christ's blood, we were bought back from slavery—redeemed from sin, a cruel slave master. We should live like free men and women, not like sharecroppers who are afraid to leave the plantation.

> Therefore do not let sin reign in your mortal body so that you obey its evil desires. Do not offer the parts of your body to sin, as instruments of wickedness, but rather offer yourselves to God, as those who have been brought from death to life; and offer the parts of your body to him as instruments of righteousness. For sin shall not be your master, because you are not under law, but under grace."
> Romans 6:12-14

Violating our bodies, God's temple, has devastating consequences.

> Don't you know that you yourselves are God's temple and that God's Spirit lives in you? If anyone destroys God's temple, God will destroy him; for God's temple is sacred, and you are that temple.
> 1 Corinthians 3:16-17

Single Christians who cannot exercise self-control are advised to marry.

> For it is better to marry than to be aflame with passion and tortured continually with ungratified desire.
> 1 Corinthians 7:9 AMPLIFIED

Married people are to be faithful.

> Marriage should be honored by all, and the marriage bed kept pure, for God will judge the adulterer and all the sexually immoral.
> Hebrews 13:4

The apostle Paul reminds us that one day, Jesus is coming back for us, his church. In this same chapter just a few verses earlier we read this admonition.

> It is God's will that you should be sanctified: that you should avoid sexual immorality; that each of you should learn how to control his own body in a way that is holy and honorable, not in passionate lust like the heathen who do not know God; and that in this matter no one should wrong his brother or take advantage of him. The Lord will punish men for all such sins, as we have already told you and warned you. For God did not call us to be impure, but to live a holy life. Therefore, he who rejects this instruction does not reject man but God, who gives you his Holy Spirit.
>
> 1 Thessalonians 4:3-8

The Bible ends with a final warning about the seriousness of sexual sin. It is not a warning to unbelievers but to the readers of this text—Christians. It isn't the *knowing* of the Word that is most important. It's the *doing* of the Word.

> Blessed are those who do His commandments, that they may have the right to the tree of life, and may enter through the gates into the city. But outside are dogs and sorcerers and sexually immoral and murderers and idolaters, and whoever loves and practices a lie.
>
> Revelation 22:14-15 NKJV

The Safety Zone

As parents keep their children from playing with fire or electrical outlets, God established sexual purity and fidelity in marriage to keep his children from the heartbreak of broken relationships, the hardships of bearing children out of wedlock, the agony of abortion, and the trauma of sexually transmitted disease. Marriage is the safety zone in which mutually faithful husbands and wives enjoy sexual intercourse free from such worries.

The task of keeping kids sexually pure is impossible without teaching biblical principles. Giving children, preteens, and teens the tools to make wise decisions is an educational process.

It's the fourth R. Not only must we teach our children reading, 'riting, and 'rithmetic, but we must also teach our children *reasoning*. We need to equip our daughters and sons to think from a biblical perspective and therefore have a Christian worldview. As we teach our children, we give them the tools—and rules—to obey God and make wise decisions for their lives.

chapter 2

the privilege of parenting

Behold, children are a heritage from the LORD,
The fruit of the womb is a reward.
Like arrows in the hand of a warrior,
So are the children of one's youth.
Happy is the man who has his quiver full of them;
They shall not be ashamed,
But shall speak with their enemies in the gate.
Psalm 127:3-5 NKJV

Birth announcements adorned with bows and ribbons spotlight the new parents' enormous gratitude for the gift of their child. Anyone who has waited for the news that they are pregnant understands that the blessing of children is never to be taken for granted. Parenting is an awesome privilege.

* * *

It was Friday night. The social worker was due to arrive Monday morning, and with precision timing, I was just completing the final class that qualified me to be a foster mother. The road to getting my niece from New York to

Los Angeles had been long and arduous, particularly because she had lived in Chicago before becoming a ward of the state, which meant that three states (Illinois, New York, and California) and miles and miles of paperwork were involved. Finally, the frustrating journey was about to end.

"Keep the refrigerator stocked with food. And, by the way, when the social worker comes to do your site visit, make sure you have a separate bed for the child."

My celebration ceased. A separate bed? I was single and lived in a furnished studio apartment. There was only one single bed and no extra room, not even for a tiny cot. I had planned to camp out on the floor with my sleeping bag until we were able to move, but that was later on down the line. For now, all I wanted was to get this child out of the system.

A separate bed? "What will happen if there's only one bed?" I asked.

"Your site visit will be rescheduled to a later date when you can demonstrate that you have room for the child."

More time? More paperwork? It had taken months to get to this point, and the thought of starting all over again left me in stunned silence. On the drive home, my hands tightly grasped the top of the steering wheel as I hunched forward, straining to see the road ahead of me as if the answer would be lying there.

I talked to God out loud. "Okay, Father. Now what? I know that getting La Nej is what you want me to do. But what now? How am I going to get an extra bed into that tiny studio and make it look ready for a child by Monday? What on earth am I going to do in two days?"

When I arrived home, I was assaulted with the unthinkable. The rancid stench of sewer attacked my nostrils. My neighbor was in the hall hysterical. Pipes had burst somewhere in the walls, and our ground floor studios were flooded with . . . *excrement!*

I opened the door to my apartment and dodged chunks of dark brown feces washing over the industrial brown carpet. My mind silently screamed, "Lord, not only do I not have a bed, but now my apartment reeks!" I began picking up everything that lay in the way of this stinking surge oozing from a hole in the bathroom wall.

"How can you remain so calm?" my neighbor asked.

"All things work together for good," was the only explanation that came from my lips. "In all things, God is working together for my good." I repeated this over and over as I dashed to the computer to rescue my writing and to the closet to retrieve my shoes. It was now about 10:00 p.m., and the smell was stifling. I wondered how impressed the social worker would be when she got a whiff of this! How would I get the stench out of the carpet in time?

But now, this is what the LORD says—
    he who created you, O Jacob,
    he who formed you, O Israel:

    "Fear not, for I have redeemed you;
    I have summoned you by name; you are mine.
    When you pass through the waters,
    I will be with you;
    and when you pass through the rivers,
    they will not sweep over you."

Isaiah 43:1-2

The waters referred to here are not clear, sparkling waters. They are dirty, murky, smelly waters. I was standing in Isaiah 43!

Moments later two security guards were at my door apologizing profusely. My neighbor's apartment had a little mess, but hers came from the overflow flushing across the hall from my studio.

"We'll get this place cleaned up, but meanwhile we don't expect you to sleep here tonight," they said. "There's an apartment upstairs where you can spend the night."

I followed the guards numbly up to the second floor. On the way, one guard suggested that since it would require much time to clean my studio, perhaps they could talk to management about moving me into this apartment immediately. I agreed. Since it was right above me, I expected another studio, but when the door opened, I was standing in the middle of a miracle. It was a furnished two-bedroom, two-bathroom apartment with a view!

The guards moved me in that night, and friends came to help with books and the rest of the items on Saturday. Through yet another miracle, management switched my telephone to the new apartment on that same day. After getting settled, I went to the mall to purchase children's posters, a few throw pillows, and jewelry boxes to add a child's touch to the bed and bathroom.

When the social worker called on Monday morning to confirm that she was on her way, she asked, "Apartment 101?" I corrected her, "No. Apartment 201." She stayed less than five minutes. "This is beautiful. Everything is in order. I'll approve you immediately." With that, the inspection was completed.

"Who is this child," I wondered, "that God would intervene so for her? And who am *I* that he trusts me so?"

* * *

Is every parent in such awe? Counting fingers and toes, checking ears and eyes could hold no more wonder than what I had experienced. God trusts me. And God trusts you. Imagine that! He has given you and me the privilege of raising *his* children.

Psalm 127 (see the epigraph at the beginning of this chapter) tells us that children are our heritage. Everyone wants an inheritance, a substantial possession that is destined to earn big rewards. Children are our inheritance. They are allotted to us by God, but first they are his. He lends them to us "as a man entrusts his fortune to his heirs."[1] Like any inheritance, children are investments designed to produce benefits.

The quiver is a case for holding arrows. Happy is the man whose quiver is full of children. Arrows are aimed in a particular direction and used for a specific purpose. Primarily, arrows are instrumental in helping warriors obtain food and protect property. Children are our arrows. We aim them in the areas of ministry, business, government, and private enterprise, where they will generate dividends for heaven's sake. That these children speak with their enemies in the city gate implies that the enemies get this far and no further.

Never is a child born who is a mistake. Regardless of the circumstances of birth, each child is destined by God and born on purpose—God's purpose. When we acknowledge this fact, we will handle our inheritances with great care. Raising children to be sexually pure begins with understanding that we have been entrusted with treasures, and we will treat them accordingly. Valuing our children and respecting them is the first step in raising godly offspring.

We're Big, They Aren't

God's wisdom is amazing. He designed parents with a generation gap in mind. We have more experience; we're supposed to be wiser. In other words, we're big, and our children aren't.

How easy it is to ignore simple requests, to dismiss tiny worries. In the quest to be good parents, we often move so fast that we don't take time to listen. Barking demands, always saying no because that's the quickest response, and being too tired to enter our child's world are symptoms of parenting by proxy. We're going through the motions, but we aren't really present for our children. Our needs are greater; our wants come first. Of course, no good father or mother would ever admit such, but we scream this truth when we're too busy to pay attention.

* * *

One of the items that survived the move from New York to Los Angeles was La Nej's treasured doll, Pillow Person, a present from Mrs. Mallory, La Nej's fifth-grade teacher. She remembers that Mrs. Mallory often wore a long, black fur coat to class and that her husband was a doctor. A memorable teacher, Mrs. Mallory went out of her way to demonstrate trust in her students, and she gave La Nej her first classroom assignment. It was evident that she taught for the love of it, and because of the relationship, Pillow Person was a cherished memento.

Pillow Person was a pillow shaped like a person. She had hair, a face with eyes, nose, and mouth, ears, arms, legs, and a down-stuffed body—the better to snuggle with! Pillow Person traveled well. She liked riding in cars, would go camping without complaint, and was as "draggable" as she was huggable. Without a doubt, Pillow Person was the third member of our family.

One day Pillow Person had to face the suds. She couldn't go another moment without spinning in the washing machine. La Nej reluctantly agreed, and in Pillow Person went. I was in my bedroom, and La Nej was folding the clothes. All of a sudden, there La Nej was at my door, quite distraught and holding Pillow Person, who had come slightly apart and lost some of her stuffing. A doctor might have diagnosed "washer-dryer syndrome." It wasn't major, really. A few stitches, and she would be back to normal.

"I'll sew her in a minute," I said, thinking I was teaching a lesson in patience. I don't even remember what I was doing at the time.

Teary-eyed, my daughter demanded that I fix Pillow Person *now*. I smiled and said again, "In a minute," and went back to my important nothing.

When I finally emerged ready to handle my daughter's crisis, I was shocked to learn that she had taken the situation into her own hands. In her mind, Pillow Person was ruined, so she marched down to the dumpster and threw Pillow Person away.

I ran downstairs to retrieve this cherished doll, but to my dismay, she was nowhere to be found. Just that quickly, the trash had been collected. I ran out to the street to see if I could catch the truck. The street was empty. Pillow Person was gone forever.

* * *

My daughter later thought that *she* had learned the lesson and blamed Pillow Person's demise solely on herself. She would often chastise herself by saying, "That's what I get for being so dramatic!"

But it was I who learned an important lesson that day. What might have happened had I understood my child's distress? What was so important that I couldn't cry with her, leave what I was doing, and mend Pillow Person right away? Why did I see this crisis from the standpoint of a big person and not from the heartache of a little girl whose doll was coming apart? Was I on the phone? Was I writing? Reading? I can't even remember what I was doing that was so important.

The saying, "A stitch in time saves nine," had new meaning for me. I mourned Pillow Person's loss and wished that I had sewn a stitch in time. Whenever my daughter missed Pillow Person, I ached inside. Every time she went to sleep and told herself it was her own fault that Pillow Person was gone, I was reminded that I was not there when she needed me, that I had not been sensitive to her pain. I vowed not to forget the difference between listening and hearing.

R-E-S-P-E-C-T

That great rhythm and blues artist Aretha Franklin challenged: "R-E-S-P-E-C-T. Find out what it means to me."

Respect for our children means that we do all we can to see the world from their point of view. Isn't that what Jesus did for us? Rather than showing up on earth full-grown, which certainly might seem more expedient, Jesus humbled himself and became a baby. He was a toddler. He learned to walk. He fell down. He lost his baby teeth. The master of the universe loves us so much that he stooped down to our level.

Sexual purity begins with respect, which is modeled by parents to their children. If parents don't respect their children, the children won't learn to respect themselves. Letting children know that they are valued can be demonstrated in many different ways. A space of their own—a bed, a room—that is respected will eventually translate to a body that is treated with respect. Listening to our children (and *hearing* them!), complimenting their efforts, understanding their pain, and allowing them to express their emotions in healthy ways all communicate respect.

"Speak when you're spoken to. Come when you're called. Come like a child, or don't come at all." So goes the oft-repeated mantra heard by many children of my era. A child's place is a child's place. While this may be somewhat true, a certain superiority is implied. Feeling "bigger than" may also make some feel "better than." Perhaps this is why we've allowed abortion to destroy so many millions of tiny lives. Abortion, child abuse, sexual abuse, and cruelty to children are the ugly, distorted by-products of the strong exercising their power over the weak. Jesus offers this warning to those who dare to harm the young:

> But if anyone causes one of these little ones who believe in me to sin, it would be better for him to have a large millstone hung around his neck and to be drowned in the depths of the sea.
>
> Matthew 18:6

(A millstone was a four-foot wide concrete wheel used for grinding in the Middle East. This is serious judgment!)

When parents respect their children, they consider their children's needs to be as important as their own. Answering a request, however, may not be convenient.

* * *

Shelly was exhausted. Between teaching part time and parenting two children full time, she seemed always to be running to catch up with her schedule despite a helpful and fully engaged husband. Once at home with her daughter, she breathed deeply, ready for a half hour of calm before it was time to pick up her son, Ryan.

"Mom, can we go to the park?" Two-year-old Brittany was tugging at her resolve. Shelly looked at her child and at the bouncy blonde curls framing blushed cherub cheeks.

"It's not very windy today." Shelly offered this explanation, fully understanding the why behind this request. Brittany had a brand new kite, and she wanted to see it fly.

"Please, Mommy!" Brittany's plea was loud enough for a listening mother to hear. Kissing her half-hour rest good-bye, Shelly swooped up Brittany and the kite and headed right back out the door, into the car, and off to the park.

There really *wasn't* enough wind, but the anticipation in Brittany's eyes was enough to warm the heart of God. Shelly desperately prayed aloud, "God, please send the wind!" The breeze came from nowhere, picked up the kite, and off they ran for a few laugh-filled minutes. It was an eternity for Brittany, but ultimately it was not flying the kite that held her in awe.

She had heard her mother pray and had seen God answer.

"God sent the wind!" Brittany said as she wiggled back into her car seat. "Thank you, Mommy!"

* * *

How to Listen

Listening is an art. The person who listens is the only person worth talking to. If parents want to be listened to, they must first learn how to listen.

1. *Stop what you're doing.* Turn off the water and stop washing the dishes. Turn off the television. Turn off the radio. Stand still. Stop!

2. *Get down to your child's eye level.* Walk into your child's room. Sit on the floor. Hold your child on your lap. Get face to face so you can see eye to eye. Turn your full body toward the person who is talking. Lean forward.

3. *Don't interrupt.* Keep quiet. Don't speak during the pregnant pause. Wait for it to birth your child's sentiment. Don't finish the sentence; wait until it is said completely. Don't rush the process.

4. *Hear the emotion.* Listen from the heart. Don't minimize. Try to grasp the feeling. Is it hurt, confusion, doubt, insecurity, rejection, or loneliness? Think, *"If this were happening to me, I would feel . . ."* Ask, "Are you feeling . . . ?"

5. *Listen with your eyes.* Listen eye to eye. Look past the words. Notice body language. Catch telling actions like slumped shoulders, tight jaws, and watery eyes.

6. *Hear what's not being said.* Don't miss the obvious. Don't be fooled by appearances.

7. *Empathize.* Feel what your child is feeling. Try to remember when something similar happened to you.

8. *Restate what you've heard.* Put into your own words what you've just heard and give your child a chance to correct you. Say it again. Add the feeling.

9. *Don't spiritualize.* Avoid using a scriptural Band-Aid. Listen, really listen *first.* Restate. Add the feeling. Wait for more.

10. *Don't give advice.* Resist the urge to tell your child what to do. Allow for a different perspective. It's all right not to immediately have the answer. It's more than all right just to listen.

Really listening is called *attending* and *active listening.* It is an art form that we should practice daily. Listen to the person at the checkout counter, to your neighbor down the street, to the cat who wants to be petted, to the birds chirping praises to God.

Some say that communication is key to keeping kids sexually pure. True, but communication is not just *talking.* Communication is *listening.* The person who said that perhaps God gave us two ears and only one mouth so that we can listen twice as much as we speak was probably right.

> My dear brothers, take note of this: Everyone should be quick to listen, slow to speak.
>
> James 1:19

Family Listening Exercise

Who is your child's best friend?
What is your child's greatest fear?
What is your child's greatest dislike?
What has been your child's most serious disappointment?
Do you know your child's favorite color? food? activity? book? artist? movie? Scripture?
What are your child's hopes?
What most hurts your child's feelings?
What are your child's dreams for the future?
If anything could be changed in the world, what would your child change, and why?
How many questions can you find answers to by really listening?

God Listens

Every parent who has ever cried, "Help!" needs to know that God is listening. He is our Abba Father, which translates into "Dear Daddy." As our parent, he is ever present to guide us, to provide for us, and to protect us. Having a relationship with an earthly father who is a *real* daddy helps us understand the value and importance of having a relationship with our heavenly Father. There is a difference between knowing one has a dad and personally knowing that dad.

"Be still, and know that I am God" (Ps. 46:10).

Rise early and read your Bible. Take time to listen to the Scriptures as they speak God's will for your day. Be still enough to hear God's voice. Take a moment to reflect. Hear the emotions of the Scriptures. Look up words. Dig deeper than the surface. Read again, aloud. Listen and hear God's Word.

Journaling is a wonderful way to listen. It is both educational and therapeutic. Write down the gist of what you've read. Write down what you feel. Write down how God feels. Write out your prayer. Now be still.

Without earthly fathers—or father figures—it may be difficult for children to grasp the compassionate, caring nature of God the Father, the omnipotent God who is strong yet gentle enough to gather us under his wings. Fathers have a vital role in keeping their children sexually pure. They are often intuitive about danger while their spouses tend to be less guarded or even naive. Kids are often more careful about breaking guidelines set by their dad, especially when they have to come home to face him. A dad's presence in his children's lives offers balance and security.

* * *

Throughout high school my niece, La Nelle, had a crush on a boy at church. But her father, Allen, felt differently about this boy. "Stay away from him," was his stern advice.

One evening when her father arrived to pick her up from choir rehearsal, he saw this boy leaning on La Nelle's shoulders. "Get away from her," he commanded. The boy jumped. La Nelle was never allowed to talk to him again. The crush soon faded, and she is now attending a Christian college.

"I'm glad my dad protected me," she says. "That boy now has two children out of wedlock. Dad saw something in his character that I didn't see." And with a precious smile she adds, "I trust my dad."

Who Needs a Husband?

The headline of a national weekly news magazine was startling. "Who Needs a Husband?" the cover story blared. "More women are saying no to marriage and embracing the single life. Are they happy?" asked the subtitle. The article overwhelmingly asserted that single women answer, "Yes, we're doing just fine, thank you!" Interestingly, however, 78 percent of the women in this same article said they thought they eventually would find the perfect mate and marry.[2] The "I'm okay. I don't need a man," knee-jerk reaction is highlighted in the article, but the numbers speak differently. The overwhelming majority of single women in America still want to marry.

Why? Because we *do* need men! That's how God designed us.

* * *

I turned off the freeway and headed back to the church. I was not quite through with talking to God. That morning we had just completed a three-day prayer conference. We had been taught to pray the Scriptures, and there was one more Scripture I wanted to wave across the balcony of heaven.

The janitor was cleaning the church but said that I would not interrupt him if I prayed in the prayer chapel. I was grateful. On my knees, I opened my Bible to Genesis 2:18, a verse one of my professors had recently explained: "The LORD God said, 'It is not good for the man to be alone. I will make a helper suitable for him.'"

"Man" in this verse refers not to man as in male, but to humankind as in male and female. God said that it is not good for humankind to be alone, and that includes women, which included me.

I opened my large Bible, and with both hands lifted it high and held it above my head. I wanted God to peer over his throne, read these words, and remember what he had said. "See, Father?" I asked him. "*You* said it's not good for humankind to be alone. And I agree! It's not good for me to be alone any longer!"

I told God every reason why I needed a husband. The very long list began with my daughter. How could she grow up without having a relationship with a father? I had been very close to my dad; he was my hero. Every relationship I'd ever had with a male had been measured by the standards my dad modeled. I couldn't imagine what life would be like without him. Perhaps this was magnified in my mind's eye because for much of my childhood my birth mother was unable to care for us; dad was both mother and father.

La Nej needed a father. I needed a husband. My hormones were raging, and yes, I told God so! I had presented my body to him according to Romans 12:1-2, but I was still living inside of his temple that he designed, so I knew he understood exactly what I meant. I told God about the financial pressures of being a single mom. It was one thing to be broke by myself, but when I was broke with another mouth to feed, now that was pressure. I was constantly in a state of worrying about not worrying about money. I needed help.

Additionally, God was calling me into ministry. How could I be a single woman in ministry? I know that for some women this is not a problem, but it wasn't a tune to which I particularly wanted to dance. *I* needed a husband.

This was the first time I didn't tell God what my husband should look like. I didn't care how tall he was or whether he had an athletic build, pot belly, or bald head. My criteria were whittled down to only two requests. "Father, let him love his wife as Christ loved the church," was the first request. I knew that God would agree with this because it is what he said in Ephesians 5:25. "And please, let him be a praying man." This second request was a throwback to the most precious memories of my own father. As a child, I was often ill. My dad would pray for me morning, noon, or in the middle of the night, in the hospital, wherever. I'm healed today because my daddy anointed my head with oil and prayed for me. I wanted most of all a man who knew how to wrestle with God in prayer.

Here I was, never married and forty-one years old. Until I committed my life to God ten years earlier, I was a magnet for losers. Now I had been waiting to be found, because "he who finds a wife finds what is good and receives favor from the LORD" (Prov. 18:22).

"Father," I added to my prayer, "let my husband *find* me." In preparation I had asked God years before to make me look like a wife. I didn't want to look like a girlfriend or a plaything, but when my husband looked at me, he would see his wife. "God, make me a wife," had been a daily prayer long before I actually met my husband.

I began to dress like a wife, walk like a wife, talk like a wife, think like a wife. My clothing became more and more modest. I didn't socialize in places where wives wouldn't be, didn't go out looking for a husband. I was waiting to be found and, yes, wanting God to speed up the process!

That was it. I didn't ask for more. I don't know how I ended up at this next passage. Maybe I was referencing the word "acceptable" in Romans 12:2 (KJV). All I know is that these words were echoed from God's sacred pages to my heart's ears. I knew that God listened, and I knew that he had heard.

> "In the time of my favor I heard you,
> and in the day of salvation I helped you."
> I tell you, now is the time of God's favor,
> now is the day of salvation.
>
> 2 Corinthians 6:2

It has been said that waiting for God's will is like sitting in a parked car. We're in the car but going absolutely nowhere. The motor isn't even turned on. Then, all of a sudden, we're racing down the freeway at ninety miles an hour!

That's how God's will manifested in my life. A week after my earnest prayer, a man I had met at a retreat asked me to go to a concert with him. I turned him down because I had to study.

"What if I call you back in a couple of hours and see how much reading you've accomplished?" said Irving.

"Okay," I said.

"Mommy, go out," La Nej pleaded when I got off the phone. "You never go anywhere." Perhaps I was embarrassed that she had noticed. I'm not sure how much reading I completed waiting for the phone to ring again. When Irving called the second time, I agreed to go on a date with him after church that Sunday.

We were engaged to be married three weeks later. We flew to New York so that he could meet my dad, and Irving was the only date my father ever liked. Our wedding was set for ten months later, Saturday, June 9,

1990. La Nej was a part of the ceremony, and later Irving and I officially adopted her. We are family.

* * *

When we are his, God fulfills our heart's desires because we desire what he desires us to desire. Not all women desire to be married, which is fine. But such decisions cannot be imposed upon others. Children need fathers.

For the Kids' Sake

Being together and staying married for the children's sake helps to keep kids sexually pure. *Keeping* is a process, and in most cases, it takes two. The Institute for Youth Development published research from the National Longitudinal Study of Adolescent Health (Add Health), examining the role of children's connectedness to parents and avoidance of unhealthy risk behavior.[3] It reports on family structure using the following categories: two biological parents or adoptive parents; biological mom and stepdad; biological dad and stepmom; single mom; single dad; and surrogate parent.

This study found that adolescents living with two biological or adoptive parents are least likely to engage in sexual intercourse. Those living with surrogate parents are more likely to experiment sexually. The next family structures in which kids are most likely to have sex are those in which adolescents live with a single dad or with a biological mom and stepdad. Finally, children living with a single mom or with a biological dad and stepmom are the next most likely to have sex.

Just because children are raised in single-parent homes does not automatically mean they will be sexually active. It does mean, however, that these parents will have to guard against any influence that negatively impacts their children. Modeling in the home is a strong conveyor of sexual information, and parents are the most important models in their children's lives.

Behavior that is in concert with biblical principles and models fidelity to God will positively impact all children. Since experimental, unconventional ways have proven not to work, it is time to get back to basics.

In other words, single people living together without being married or cohabiting—as it's called because of convenience, financial benefits, or any other excuse—are modeling poor values to their children. Research shows that children who live with people who are cohabiting are more likely to become sexually active. By contrast, children of married parents are more likely to remain virgins. Next are children who live with single parents who don't cohabit. (See Figure, "Family Structure and Teen Virginity").

Married couples that stay together in fidelity and single parents who live holy are the best teachers of sexual purity. Remember, your children are paying attention to what you say . . . but more attention to how you live.

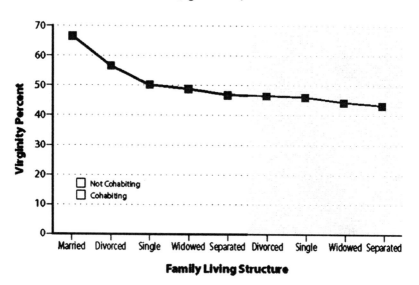

Family Structure and Teen Virginity
(ages 12–17)

Source: NLS Add Health   Calculations by Pat Fagan, The Heritage Foundation

Dangers of Divorce

Today, divorce is a societal norm, but it may be a precursor for adolescent nonmarital sexual activity. One study demonstrates that while 57 percent of virgins come from homes where families remain intact, the majority of boys who are promiscuous are from homes where there is divorce, remarriage, and repartnering.[4]

Divorce means that one parent is gone, and that's usually the father. Moms are more often than not raising the children alone. Dads in the home diminish kids' delinquent behavior. In fact, delinquency is twice as high when dads are absent.[5] A father's presence can provide daughters with a stable relationship with a nonexploitative adult male who loves and respects them. Security and trust derived from this relationship help girls avoid precocious sexual activity and exploitative relationships with other males. Fathers contribute to core aspects of children's stability, self-confidence, self-regulation, and self-identity in profound ways.[6]

* * *

Richard Durfield, the model dad who brought family chastity pledges to the forefront as told in *Focus on the Family*, shared how he and his wife presented a promise ring to each of their children, who in turn wore the rings as a promise to remain sexually pure. This inspired my husband, Irving.

We ordered a chastity necklace and took La Nej out for dinner when she was fourteen. After dinner Irving held the necklace in its dainty box and told his daughter about the importance of keeping herself sexually pure. He explained to her that God expects obedience, and he reviewed once again that sex was designed for marriage only. Then he told La Nej that as her parents we expected her to obey the Lord and to obey us.

"We want you to promise us that you will keep yourself sexually pure," he said. He did not lecture as much as he entreated. He spoke deliberately, as if he wanted her to remember every word.

My heart brimmed with pride and gratitude as I watched my husband talk to La Nej. Silently I thanked God for this godly man.

"I promise," she said.

"We're giving you this necklace, and we want you to wear it every day as a reminder of your promise." He took the gold necklace out of its box and with ceremonial gesture clasped it on her neck.

La Nej smiled proudly. She loved the attention from her dad, and she cherished the feeling that she was very, very special to both of us. La Nej knew that how she lived her life and treated her body were of supreme importance. The necklace was lost in gym class after a year or so, but the memory of that night—and the promise she made—was never forgotten.

* * *

Parents who present a united front model commitment to their children. Seeing dad and mom living together as a married couple provides a necessary blueprint that solidifies the sexual purity message.

In *The Unexpected Legacy of Divorce*, authors Wallerstein, Lewis, and Blakeslee studied a small sample of children whose parents had divorced. Wallerstein followed these children for twenty-five years to learn whether or not their parents' divorce had any lasting effects on them. The results were predictable. As adults, these children of divorce had difficulty forming committed relationships. The authors concluded that the effects of broken families are longer lasting than previously assumed. Their advice? Barring violent or abusive relationships, it's better to stay together for the kids' sake. And that, of course, is the biblical model.

There are no easy answers for couples that go through difficult times. Christian couples feel as frustrated as do non-Christians when the satisfaction curve dips in the opposite direction. But since the family is at stake, and the children's future is on the line, perhaps it's time to sit down and take one more look at the wedding video before ultimately deciding to walk out the door. Reliving the joy of that commitment may not solve the immediate problem, but it may provide enough encouragement to try one more time.

Children's security is couched in the home and in the "everydayness" of life with their parents. Men provide what women can't. And women provide what men can't. If staying together for the children's sake is the only reason to remain married, that's good enough.

chapter 3

raising God-fearers

The fear of the LORD is the beginning of wisdom,
and knowledge of the Holy One is understanding.
Proverbs 9:10

A man came upon some bricklayers and asked one, "What are you building?"

"A wall," the bricklayer wearily replied.

Then the man asked a second bricklayer, "What are you building?" The bricklayer stood strong, pointed to his growing wall of bricks, and announced proudly, "I'm building a cathedral."

It's all in the perspective. And perspective is important.

As we raise our children, we might well ask ourselves, "What am I building?" Adding clarity to our goals may give us a heavenly perspective.

* * *

I had a rude awakening the day I tried to have Bible study with my daughter. She whined, stomped her feet, and said, "Noooo!" I persisted anyway, but it didn't take long to see that all she was waiting for was our time in the Word to be over.

I've known families who had devotions together. Some dear friends of mine discovered that their daughter was gifted when at three years old she had memorized and could recite an entire chapter verbatim that her father had read to her the night before.

Why wasn't this working for me? The only result I could see was that La Nej was resenting the very thought of a formal Bible study. She would rather talk than read. But how would she ever really know God?

The Deuteronomy 6:7 passage came to mind. I had to "talk" to her when we sat at home, walked along the road, lied down, and got up. I had to capitalize on our time together. And I had to be a living example of God's Word. Telling her Bible accounts ("This reminds me of David and Goliath . . ." and "That's similar to what happened in the book of Esther . . ."), using every teachable moment, and modeling Christ replaced my attempts at formal Bible study.

One day La Nej was grounded, but a certain store was having a sale, and I wanted to go shopping. Since I couldn't leave her home alone, I cautioned that although she was going with me, *I* would be the only one shopping. We went into the mall, and I headed for the store's sale rack. My daughter also headed for the sale rack. She found a sunflower yellow dress sprinkled with daises. She tried it on. It fit beautifully. I pretended to ignore her until she asked me to buy the dress for her. Here was a teachable moment.

"What is the definition of mercy?" I asked. She looked blank.

"Mercy is when God *doesn't* give us what we *do* deserve," I explained. I asked her to repeat this definition, explaining that when she deserved a spanking but didn't get one, that was mercy.

"What is the definition of grace?" Again I was met with a blank stare. "Grace is when God *does* give us what we *don't* deserve." I asked her to repeat this definition. "The Lord Jesus Christ gives us salvation. We can't earn it, and we certainly don't deserve it. I am going to buy you this dress even though you don't deserve it. Every time you put it on, I hope it reminds you of God's grace to all of us."

On my own, I continued with my personal early morning devotions. In our home, lights were out at 9:00 p.m., and I rose at 5:00 a.m. for an hour's study with a cup of coffee.

One morning I slept late, until 5:30 or so. When I went to my usual spot at the kitchen table, there La Nej was, sitting in my seat and reading her Bible with a cup of tea! She flashed a big smile that said, "I'm just like Mommy." She continues to read her Bible to this day.

The Reverential Fear of God

Imagine raising an army of God-fearers! Sexual purity begins with teaching children the reverential fear of God. Whether or not we realize it, we are teaching our children all of the time, so it is important for us to model Christ. Actions do speak louder than words.

As the guardians of our homes, it is our duty to impress upon our children the truths of God's Word. We accomplish this not by quoting Scripture all the time, but by fleshing out biblical principles. It's called *integration*. We think Christian; therefore we live Christian. God's truth is experienced and evident in our lives. For our children, the reality of what it means to be a Christian becomes so real that the imprint of Christ is etched in their character.

To fear God does not mean to be afraid of him, to have a sense of dread or terror that results from intimidation. To fear God means to *respect* him. An army of God-fearers—children who respect God—is an awesome goal. And we *are* building such an army, one family at a time.

Respect or reverence for God is rooted in love and key to obedience. God's great initiative to love us inspires us to love him back.

> For God so loved the world that he gave his one and only Son, that whoever believes in him shall not perish but have eternal life. For God did not send his Son into the world to condemn the world, but to save the world through him.
>
> John 3:16-17

God the Father gave his Son, Jesus Christ, to save us. Because of Adam's sin, humankind inherited a sin nature. The word *sin* means to "miss the mark." It's the picture of someone trying to hit a bull's-eye and missing every time. That's us. We try to make right decisions, but apart from God's power in our lives, we miss the bull's-eye. We may succeed at accomplishing some things, and we may even do other things well. But on the whole, without God, the grand equation of our lives adds up to meaninglessness. Because of our sin nature, we are living, but we aren't really *alive*.

Jesus Christ, the express image of God, gave his life in payment for our sin. It can be explained like this. Let's say that we've accumulated a stack of parking tickets that adds up to much more than the balance in our bank account. We come before the judge, and he's about to send us to jail, but our attorney interrupts to say that he has paid all of the parking tickets with his own funds. Who wouldn't have a heart full of gratitude for such an attorney?

This is why we love Jesus so. When we stand before God the Father, we're not standing there perfect as if we've never sinned. We've all made bad decisions; we've fallen short just as Romans 3:23 says. But Jesus, our advocate or attorney, "testifies" that he paid the entire debt for our sin with his blood on Calvary. Because of his sacrifice, we are acquitted.

By receiving Jesus as our Lord and Savior, we exchange our sinful nature for his sinless nature. We experience God's love and awaken to the dayspring of a brand-new life. We are forgiven, cleansed, made whole. The result? We love him, because he has already proven his love for us.

> But God demonstrates his own love for us in this: While we were still sinners, Christ died for us.
>
> Romans 5:8

While we were doing our own thing and shaking our fist at God, he decided to die for us. He redeemed us, bringing us back from the enemy's camp and setting us free. Who wouldn't love a God like that? And who wants to displease the one he or she loves?

When reverential fear is the controlling motive of our lives, we have a wholesome dread of hurting God's feelings, of letting him down. This is the *fear of the Lord*, and it is the beginning of the process of becoming wise, of rightly applying what we know. And when we apply what we know about God to our lives, when we actually do what the Bible says, we experience "aha" moments of understanding and exclaim, "Oh! Now I get it!" We learn to respect God, and we teach our children to respect him, too.

We know God by studying his Word. Then we teach his Word to our children so that his Word hidden in their hearts will keep them pure and help them make right decisions.

> How can a young man keep his way pure? By living according to your word. I seek you with all my heart; do not let me stray from your commands. I have hidden your word in my heart that I might not sin against you.
>
> Psalm 119:9-11

It is amazing how many parents give their children Bibles, march them up to children's church, and hand them over to the teacher as if to say, "You teach him." This is backwards. Parents are the primary teachers and therefore must know the Bible well enough to teach it. What children learn at church should reinforce what they've already learned at home. Christian education begins at home.

It is also puzzling to see parents give children the option of going or not going to class on Sunday. Statements such as "He doesn't feel like it" or "She wants to sit with me in church" leave me wondering whether these same children make such decisions about going to school during the week.

If they don't have the option Monday through Friday, why give it to them on Sunday?

* * *

At age thirteen, my prayer partner's son decided he wanted to test his boundaries. Henry started hanging out with the wrong friends and became rebellious and disobedient. To monitor his going out and coming in, his mother, Sabrina, took away his house key. He now had to come home at a decent hour if he wanted to be let in at all. Meanwhile, she prayed fervently for him and wondered, "God, has anything I've taught him about you taken root in his life?"

The night before Mother's Day, Sabrina taught her class, which ended around 8:30 p.m., but she didn't actually leave until 8:50. On the way home, she decided that she wanted to wear a new suit on Mother's Day. So even though it was late, she spent some leisure time shopping. God was leading her up and down the aisles, she believed; and sure enough, in one aisle she found a great bargain.

After shopping, Sabrina was heading home, but she then decided that she would like to pick up a video to relax. Taking this second detour, she went by the video store and spent quite a while looking for just the right movie. She didn't arrive home until 11:00.

Meanwhile, Henry had decided to come home at 10:00, and he had been waiting for his mother to return home. He hadn't seen her since 5:30 that evening, and by 10:00 he was rather concerned. It was unusual for her to be out so late. Finally, he went to a friend's house, where he spent the night.

The next morning Henry called home. No answer. He didn't know his mom had an early morning counseling session with a client. He became frantic and started calling the rest of the family. Getting no answers, he left messages like, "Mom is missing! I haven't seen her since yesterday at five o'clock! Please call me immediately."

This son had been taught by his mom and raised in the church and had received Christ as Savior at an early age. His Christian education included learning the events of the end times. When he couldn't find his mother, he just knew she had been raptured (1 Thess. 4:16-17). He thought that he had been left behind because of his disobedience.

By the time Henry caught up with his mother, he was so relieved that Jesus had not returned and taken the church without taking him, that he stayed home all day. "It's a lesson I could not have orchestrated," Sabrina said. "Thank God for the Word of God!"

* * *

When our children have been taught about God, he will help us and correct them in creative ways. The reverential fear of the Lord is the beginning of wisdom.

Teaching Stewardship

If children learn stewardship—how to reverence God with their money, time, and talent—they will understand the basic principle that everything we have belongs to God, including their bodies. Tithing is one way to teach this principle.

> "Will a man rob God? Yet you rob me.
> "But you ask, 'How do we rob you?'
> "In tithes and offerings. You are under a curse—the whole nation of you—because you are robbing me. Bring the whole tithe into the storehouse, that there may be food in my house. Test me in this," says the LORD Almighty, "and see if I will not throw open the floodgates of heaven and pour out so much blessing that you will not have room enough for it."
>
> Malachi 3:8-10

The theological debate about whether tithing is old or new covenant and whether it is a requirement for Christians today might be a convenient excuse to hold on to our money. Often, how we handle our money is an indication of whether we honestly believe God. The tithe is where giving begins. Ten percent, or ten cents, of every dollar earned belongs to God. He gets the firstfruits (Prov. 3:9-10). The tithe pays the pastor's salary so that his or her needs can be met. It also pays church staff salaries, keeps the church lights on, supports church ministries, buys toys for the nursery and books and snacks for the children, and helps parents who are struggling financially. After the tithe, we give an offering, which can be any amount.

Parents who teach their children to pay the tithe first and to set aside an offering demonstrate that God is a priority in their lives. Children who learn to pay the tithe on their allowance or other income are learning self-control rather than spending all they get.

When we tithe even though we think we can't afford to, we demonstrate to our children that we are trusting God to take care of us—and that we have a right to expect him to do so. If we're broke, we can't afford *not* to tithe. The person struggling to make ends meet truly needs to stand under heaven's open floodgates! We test God as Scripture says to—that is, we give him an opportunity to show his ability to care for us. Our children need to see God show up. Who can take for granted that God is involved in the details of our everyday lives when we depend on him for all we have? Will God let our children down? Certainly not!

* * *

My contract with the advertising agency was over, and I was back in seminary. It didn't take long to go through the financial reserves, and soon student loans were the mainstay of our income.

We had been tithing faithfully. As a single parent, I wanted my child to trust God with her life, and where better to begin than with her money? Because I told La Nej what God expected and explained what the tithe pays for in our church, tithing was a responsibility she never questioned. We sometimes kept extra envelopes at home so that her coins could be put into them for children's church. She knew that because we tithed, God was responsible for taking care of us.

I didn't burden La Nej with problems, but I did let her know when funds were low. One time I told her that we just didn't have any more money. "Well, just go to the machine and get some!" she demanded. At times I wished it were that simple.

It was summer. School loans were spent, and I hadn't yet found a job. The rent was due, and the refrigerator was empty. I stood in front of the supermarket, looked up into the serene Californian sky, and said, "Lord, you have to take care of us! I know you didn't give me this child so that she could starve." And with that I decided to buy groceries. Afterward, I went to the bank and told the assistant manager that I'd just written a rubber check at the supermarket.

"God will show up for you," she said rather nonchalantly. Over that past year, I had been sharing my testimony with my bankers in the hope of winning them to Christ. There were three assistant managers, and they knew my struggle to get my niece to Los Angeles from New York. Every step of the way I had apprised them of the developments. With every victory I underscored that God was responsible. Now I felt a little embarrassed, but I didn't know what else to do.

"Don't worry about it. We'll take care of it." And they did. Food, rent, phone—it was a miracle that my checks cleared all summer, because I didn't have a line of credit available. When fall came and money from student loans became available, I paid up my debt.

Throughout that long summer, my daughter and I celebrated God's provision for us every step of the way. I mentioned over and over again that

God was working on our behalf because we had honored him with the tithe. It was a lesson neither of us would forget.

* * *

I do not recommend this action for anyone. I should have talked to my bankers before buying food, and I certainly would never do it again. The point of this unusual story is that when we trust God by giving him the tithe, God takes care of his own in ways we can't imagine. He gave me favor with my bankers, and often favor is better than money. The best strategy, however, is higher finance—the principle of living debt-free.[1]

Praying for and with Your Children

Prayer is essential to raising God-fearers. If we don't pray for our children, who will? Praying with them helps us hear their concerns. We encourage them to take their needs to God, then we trust God to meet those needs. Children learn to pray by hearing parents pray.

* * *

"My mom taught me how to pray and how to trust God," Nancy Kwon told me. Her mother had been raised in Korea as a Buddhist, and she was an ardent believer in Buddha until the night she went to her Christian friend's home for dinner. This friend's family had no food, but they all sat around the table and said grace. After they thanked God for the food that he was going to give them, they waited.

"My mother watched in amazement and thought that they were a little out of their minds. But after a few minutes, there was a knock at the door. A neighbor was standing there with food she wanted to share with the family. My mother accepted Jesus Christ as her Lord and Savior.

"Over the years, I learned how to pray because I heard my mother pray," says Nancy. "She had been married to my dad for eleven years, and she prayed for his salvation every day. She never complained about her husband to her parents. She told everything to God. My three sisters and I would hear her pray out loud. She believed Romans 10:11: 'Anyone who trusts in [God] will never be put to shame.' Today my father is a pastor."

* * *

When we teach our children to pray, we encourage them to trust God for themselves. Children have needs at all ages, so when presented with a "Mommy, I need . . . ," why not add it to the child's prayer list? If parents pray simple, one-sentence prayers, children will learn that praying is easy. "Father, I thank you for finding the right parking space." When God answers, celebrate him. Give God the glory.

Pray for healing, pray about purchasing a dog, pray for a "window" in heavy traffic, pray about buying the right pair of shoes, pray for the scraped knee to be healed, pray about what church to join, pray for the teacher and the coach, pray for the right friends, pray about what gift to buy, pray when something is lost—pray, pray, pray!

As children learn to pray and see answers to their prayers, God becomes even more real to them. When prayers are not answered the way they expect, they learn to accept God's no as well as his yes.

Remember the Cathedral

Keeping kids sexually pure is a day-to-day, ongoing task as the word *keeping* implies. One isolated conversation won't do, and talking alone is not enough. Keeping kids sexually pure is a process that begins with understanding who we want our children to be as adults. We are building cathedrals, not just walls.

Raising children who respect and reverence God is the goal. But we can't develop God-fearers without first knowing God ourselves. Studying God's Word so that we can teach basic principles to our children, tithing and expecting our children to tithe, and praying for and with our children are foundational. In the next chapter we will discover other essential tools.

chapter 4

tools in your toolbox

Whoever loves discipline loves knowledge,
but he who hates correction is stupid.
Proverbs 12:1

When my siblings and I were out of their sight, my grandparents never worried about us. They had plenty of eyes on the block. Every neighbor was on the lookout for someone else's kid. They scolded, chastised, and told on the adventurous and curious. If a neighbor had to spank us, we were *really* in trouble. And we could be guaranteed that another spanking was waiting for us once we arrived home.

As parents, we have many tools to assist us in the task of child-rearing. Learning to use them wisely is key to good parenting.

*　*　*

At first La Nej called me "Auntie" and then "Mommy-Auntie." One day she announced, "I'm not going to call you 'Auntie' anymore, just 'Mommy.'"

I froze. The word *Mommy* seemed so full of expectation. But it seemed that La Nej had thought about this for some time and was not waiting for my opinion. At times I became discouraged and felt as if I were doing a terrible job of mothering, and I'd say so.

"You're doing a great job!" would come the unrestrained affirmation complete with hugs. "You're a good Mommy!"

Conduct and Consequences

Good mommies and daddies help children understand that there are consequences to their actions. Learning these lessons early means that later on children will understand that promiscuity has its consequences and sexual purity has its rewards.

Consequences begin when a child is as young as two years old. Time out and being sent to bed early are consequences. Consequences need to be meted out firmly but with compassion, and they should be immediate and appropriate for the poor choice the child has made. Children should be taught that parents aren't *causing* the consequence. Rather, the consequence is waiting whenever the poor choice is made. When discipline is meted out, it is with the goal of correcting an action, never with hurting the child. This is not to say that discipline may not be uncomfortable, but discipline is never excessive, abusive, or out of control.

Good decisions bring rewards.
Poor choices bring consequences.

Repeat these phrases often and post them on the refrigerator. Let children know that they are responsible for their actions and that they affect their own future by the choices they make.

*　*　*

Every morning was a battle. "La Nej, make up your bed." In her defiant little way, she would ignore me. "I'm just going to mess it up again tonight," she'd retort. The solution to what she considered to be a meaningless task was to simply pull the spread over the rumpled sheets below.

My plan of action was strategic. *Tell* her how to make up the bed. *Show* her how to make up the bed. Make up the bed *with* her. Show her *again*. Tell her *again*. Explain why it's important. Repeat . . . .

This went on for about a year. Finally, one morning out of exasperation I blurted, "If you don't make up that bed, I'm going to give you a spanking."

"Oh, please! You're not going to spank me!" And with that assurance, she simply pulled up the top cover and stomped on her merry way.

She was right. I had avoided spanking her because I was afraid that I might cross the line from discipline to abuse. The lessons I had learned from my own mentally ill mother were still vivid even though I had lived with her for only a short period of time. The understanding and love for my mother was not enough to overcome the fear that I would react as she had reacted.

My dad had been the model of restraint. If he decided to spank us—which was twice that I remember—he would announce his intentions and then wait a while. For us, waiting was always the worst part. I didn't know then that my father was "cooling off" so that he wouldn't spank out of anger. Now, as an adult with a child of my own, I doubted that I had his self-control.

The next morning the bed was still unmade. I decided to ignore it and proceeded with my day until the Holy Spirit nudged me. I had given my word that an unmade bed equaled a spanking. Now feeling overwhelmed with the duty to follow through, I called two friends who also had children. I explained my dilemma and was assured that to spank was certainly the right decision.

Armed with their counsel but still not resolved, I turned to the Scriptures. Practical proverbs shed wisdom's light on my dilemma.

> Do not withhold discipline from a child;
>   if you punish him with the rod, he will not die.
> Punish him with the rod
>   and save his soul from death.
>
> Proverbs 23:13-14

> Folly is bound up in the heart of a child, but the rod of
>   discipline will drive it far from him.
>
> Proverbs 22:15

> The rod of correction imparts wisdom.
>   but a child left to himself disgraces his mother.
>
> Proverbs 29:15

I was convinced. When La Nej came home from school, she reminded me every few minutes about the spanking. "Are you ready to spank me yet?" she teased in her playful manner. After homework, dinner, and a bath, she put on her flannel pajamas and posed her question yet again.

"Yes, I'm ready. First, I want you to get your Bible and read these Scriptures." In addition to the Proverbs passages, I asked her to read the first Scripture that I had ever taught her.

> Children, obey your parents in the Lord, for this is right. "Honor
> your father and mother"—which is the first commandment with
> a promise—"that it may go well with you and that you may enjoy
> long life on the earth."
>
> Ephesians 6:1-3

The seriousness of what was about to take place began to settle in. Midway through her reading, La Nej began to cry, and her tears weakened my newfound resolve. But I had given my word, so without further delay it was bottoms-up with six words, "Make up your bed every morning," followed by a hug and "I love you."

The following morning the bed was made. Later, when we were in the car, La Nej broke the silence with the proclamation, "I have a strong will." Had I heard correctly? A strong will? When I was twelve, I didn't even know what having a will meant.

"Do you?" I asked. "Well, that's why God gave you to me." After that, I never again doubted the necessity of a "lick" in time.

* * *

Discipline is key. Children understand what is acceptable and what isn't when they are disciplined.

Time Out

If children don't experience the consequences of discipline early, they won't appreciate the value of consequences when they are older. Standard one-minute per age of the child time-outs are effective reminders that rules and guidelines must be obeyed.

* * *

In the church nursery a mother administered a time-out that was a beautiful model for me and the other mothers present. After several warnings, this mom removed her son from the play area and placed him in a corner and stood closely behind him. He was screaming, of course, but with her squarely behind him, he dared not move. She looked at her watch the entire time, and when two minutes were up, she picked up her son, hugged him, and returned him to the play area.

* * *

Removing privileges is an effective tool for older children. Whatever the consequence, it is imperative that parents be balanced in handling the situation. Remember, it's the action that's "bad," not the child, so the child should always be treated with respect.

The discipline must relate specifically to the infraction, and it should be reasonable. Giving month-long restrictions for a minor infraction minimizes the importance of the lesson learned. The offense is long forgotten and the child feels abused. Parents must guard against overreacting, but this doesn't mean not reacting at all.

Discipline is meaningless outside of a world of hugs, laughter, playing together, listening, talking, sharing, and in general "hanging out." It's the parent's displeasure that causes the child the greatest remorse. Children need to be loved and accepted by their parents. Most don't want to hurt their parent's feelings. Persistent problems may require counseling. A pattern of misbehaving may actually be a cry for help or attention.

When disciplining, explain why the behavior is unacceptable. Help children by asking them to suggest alternative actions that could have prevented the problem. Don't take your child's misbehaving personally. It is not intentionally meant to wound you. The saying "People do what makes sense to them at the moment" may help in seeing the world from your child's perspective so that you understand the thought processes behind the action. Sometimes kids are just testing the limits.

Quality Time

Quality time is *not* equal to quantity time. In fact, it is impossible to have quality time *without* quantity time. The early years as children are developing are critical. Parents cannot "train up a child in the way he should go" unless they are there. How else will parents understand their child's intrinsic makeup? How will they learn their child's likes and dislikes? their son's passions? their daughter's talents? How will they know what God has designed each child to be? Spending time with our children is the only way to know the answers.

* * *

"I want to be an actress," La Nej had said several times the past few weeks. Since I had never seen her act on stage, my inclination was to ignore this request. But I had just left a baby dedication class, where I had taught parents to listen to their children, so I decided to take my own advice.

"If this is God's will for you, he only has one day to do it. I'll ask for you to be excused from school on Friday, and we'll see what happens." That

Friday I scheduled a morning hair appointment for La Nej, and while we were at the salon, I began calling agencies.

"Sorry, no walk-ins," I heard again and again. "Send pictures. We'll contact you."

"I can't believe I've pulled La Nej out of school but no one will see her," I complained to my daughter's hairstylist.

"There's someone I can send you to," she said. "A friend of mine is an agent, and he's here visiting from New York. I'm sure he'll see you today."

It was a good day to see the agent. La Nej looked glamorous! Her hair was crimped and her outfit was perfect. We left the salon, and as we drove to the agent, we prayed, "Father, please open every door that needs to be open, and shut every door that needs to be shut. In Jesus' name. Amen."

After seeming to ignore us for about thirty minutes, the agent picked up the phone and made an appointment for us at one of the largest children's agencies in Los Angeles. The time was set for Monday afternoon.

"Monday! That won't work," I told him. "Her hair won't look like this on Monday!" He picked up the phone again and rescheduled our appointment. They would see us in an hour.

We prayed again before going upstairs, "Father, give us favor." In we went. I was invited to have a seat in the reception area, and La Nej was taken to a room to audition. She looked so confident. With my ears pasted to the walls, I tried to hear how the audition was going but couldn't hear anything. A few minutes later the interviewer emerged.

"Congratulations. Your daughter is *very* talented. We're signing her for print and for television. Here's a contract and a list of photographers to call for her composite."

The paperwork complete, we left the building, and both of us were amazed at God. It was 3:00 p.m. He did it in *one* day! We thanked him and then celebrated with a late lunch.

* * *

By now, the connection between valuing our children and sexual purity should be in sharper focus. If children are important to their parents, parents will treat them as if they're important. In turn, children will feel valued. If children feel valued, they will treat their bodies with respect.

Family First

Pastors, ministers, counselors, and others who work for or volunteer in the church must have this priority: family first! Placing your children above the unending demands of a needy congregation isn't easy, but it is necessary.

Many children who grow up in the church grin and bear the neglect they feel because of their mother's and/or father's involvement. Because it may seem selfish and unspiritual for them to complain, they passively acquiesce. During the teenage years, when independence sprouts its individualistic nerve, defiance may set in and children may rebel against attending church. Spending every free moment at the church can make one feel that, when given the choice, church is the last place he or she voluntarily wants to go. Kids may view the church as competition for their parents' attention. And while mom and dad are out saving the world, they may be losing their own kids.

A life of balance, doing everything decently and in order and realizing that there is a time for everything, can lend perspective to excessive religious activity. Activity, after all, doesn't make us holy; it only makes us busy. If your child is complaining, take note. Rather than leaving him or her home alone, find something you can do together. What is your child's preference? Take time to ask, "What am I running away from every time I feel the need to leave home?"

* * *

A nursery worker related this observation. "I've noticed that the less parents are involved with their children, the more needy, nagging, and clingy the children are when they're dropped off in the nursery. Some parents work a full-time job and are away from their children all day. Then they come home at night and head to church, dropping their children off at the nursery. This is more 'away' time. Children from homes like this tend to be more disruptive and demand more attention than children whose mothers are with them during the day.

"It's not just the fact that parents are working that's the issue. It's that their 'free' time—evenings and weekends—are spent on their own pursuits, their own interests and hobbies. So during the week they're involved in their career. And on weekends they're still unavailable. Their children are neglected at night, in the morning before school, and on the weekends, because even when these parents are there, they really aren't there."

Together Time

Moms and dads, stepmoms and stepdads, aunts and uncles, grandmothers and grandfathers, and foster moms and dads must be creative with finding together time beyond the chore-filled "Do this, do that" grind of daily living. Talking and listening occur during leisure time together. Enjoying athletics, a weekly movie and pizza night, reading together, and visiting museums are just a few ideas of what should be on a lengthy "things to do together" list.

Engage children in sports, music, and the arts. Learning how to play an instrument or how to swim, play tennis, golf, hockey, basketball, or soccer helps kids develop a sense of who they are, and in the process they may make discoveries about who God created them to be.

A regular daily and weekly routine helps children understand order and organization. One night of the week should be set aside for family fun. Both parents and children should look forward to this time. When a child misbehaves, taking away family night isn't a good way to discipline. In other words, if Friday night is movie night, don't use this time to discipline a child for not doing homework earlier in the week. Tie the discipline directly to the offense. It will have more meaning with longer-lasting results.

Family vacations are probably the best times for laughter. Parents who plan vacations *with* their children rather than leaving the kids behind are making investments that are guaranteed to yield dividends. There is truth in the axiom that the family that plays together stays together.

* * *

"My parents didn't treat us as inferior when we were younger," says Sonja Schappert. "We had dinner together every night, and we were included in the conversation. We talked and were listened to. Now, as an adult, I have confidence to critically think through issues and make the right decisions. The lines of communication were always open, so the foundation to talk about anything is already there. My parents communicated what they expected of me as a child of God and as their daughter—to remain sexually pure."

Sonja spoke of the special moments in junior high and high school when she and her dad went on father-daughter dates. "We didn't talk about anything in particular. It was just special spending time together. My dad would take me out to dinner and to different concerts." What Sonja valued most was finding common interest in something they could do together.

* * *

Together times are excellent opportunities to be alert to teachable moments—moments when your child is ready to learn. Fathers model to their daughters how young ladies should be treated. Mothers can take their son on dates too and teach them how to treat a lady.

When together in the car, rather than turning off the radio because the music and lyrics hurt your ears, why not listen, really listen? Ask your child what the song is saying and talk about what it means. Are the lyrics telling listeners to do anything contrary to God's Word? After this discussion, if your child doesn't voluntarily switch the station, then you be the parent and turn it off.

Monitor the television. Limit the time children spend watching TV, and by all means, be selective when you do turn it on. Television is the worst baby-sitter. It will invade your home and impose its sexual images and irresponsible ideas without your permission or consent. Children left home alone with television are exposed to the dregs of our society. The less time in front of the TV the better. Unfortunately, as we technologically advance, there is more and more monitoring to do.

* * *

Rita told me about her friend's son who had a computer in his bedroom and became involved with pornography through the Internet. When Rita purchased a computer for her own sons, she decided not to make her friend's mistake. Rather than putting the computer in the bedroom, she placed it in the living room where all the family gathered. She also employed filtering devices to help protect her boys.

* * *

Filtering devices shield children when they're online, but parents still must monitor. Smut invades our homes through unsolicited email. And since the American Library Association supports the right of children to access pornography on the Internet, children should not be left alone at the library. Unsupervised time is always a breeding ground for mischief. Parents must be actively involved in everything their children do.

Rewards and Promises

Giving rewards and keeping promises signal two things. First, rewarding good behavior says that you've paid attention long enough to notice. Second, keeping promises says that you are a person of your word.

Find something positive to say to your child every day. The compliment should be sincere and should not be tied only to the way your child looks. Always telling children that they are cute or handsome places the focus on their outward appearance when it's what's inside that counts. Find other qualities like honesty, dependability, initiative, perseverance, and so on. Praise your child for her talent, for her loyalty to friends, for her ability to make good decisions. And praise him too for his helpfulness, thoughtfulness, and good manners. Find different ways to say "I love you" every day. Reward your child with hugs, special treats, and public acknowledgment. Kids love to hear their parents bragging about them.

Keeping promises is part of developing trust. If children can't trust their parents' words, they are more likely to have difficulty trusting the Word of the heavenly Father. Disappointment is discouraging, and being constantly disappointed is destructive to any relationship. Furthermore, if parents don't keep their promises, why should children keep theirs?

Keeping Good Company

Surround your kids with the people *you* want them to be with. You be the one to decide who influences their lives. This demands that you know your children's friends and their parents and what they value. Teach your children this Scripture and say it to them often.

> Do not be misled: "Bad company
> corrupts good character."
> 1 Corinthians 15:33

Help children evaluate their friendships by causing them to realize the difference between friends who like them because of what they can get and friends who truly value them for who they are. As kids mature, this will translate into relationships with so-called girlfriends and boyfriends who say, "I love you," when what they really mean is "I love me. And I love you for what you do for me."

No matter how wonderful you consider the family next door to be, or how special the neighbors down the block are, be cautious about allowing your children to sleep anywhere but at home in their own beds. Too many children spend the night at a friend's house and are taken advantage of when no one's looking.

And the homes of family members may not be safe either. A lot of sexual abuse occurs within families. Teach your children that no one should touch them in ways that make them feel uncomfortable. Ask your children questions often, and believe them when they confide in you. Better yet, *be there* so that you'll know firsthand what's going on with your child.

* * *

My daughter La Nej says: "My mom surrounded me with mentors, Christian women in whom I could confide. At times when I didn't want her advice, I'd call one of my mentor friends to see what she thought. Because they were people my mother picked to be my 'aunties' and 'godmothers,' she felt safe that their advice would mirror her own. And she was right. It's great to have another voice saying the same thing as your mother. It is sometimes easier to hear from someone outside of my parents. But it's also great not to hear it only from your mother.

"The rules in our house were clear. It didn't matter what any of my friends did. My mom never, never allowed me to spend the night at anyone else's home. Never! Friends could spend the night at our house, but I could never spend the night at theirs. That was understood from the beginning. It was something I never questioned, because that's just the way it was."

* * *

Discipline, quantity time, prioritizing family, scheduling together time, giving rewards, keeping promises, surrounding your children with godly mentors, teaching stewardship, and praying for your children are just a few tools for healthy relationships between parents and their children. You may already have these in your toolbox in addition to others. In the next chapter, we will examine specific ways to help children build strong character—character that will help them stay sexually pure.

Tools in Your Toolbox

- Setting the goal of developing God-fearers
- Knowing God personally
- Studying the Bible
- Teaching biblical principles to your children
- Giving the tithe to God
- Praying for and with your children
- Exercising discipline
- Giving quality time
- Prioritizing family
- Giving rewards
- Keeping promises
- Providing godly mentors
- Teaching stewardship

chapter 5

at every stage

For precept must be upon precept, precept upon precept,
Line upon line, line upon line,
Here a little, there a little.
Isaiah 28:10 NKJV

When it comes to sex, most parents are confused about what to say and where to begin.

*   *   *

"Son, promise me that when you grow up, you will be abstinent," said Shawyne to her four-year-old son, Jaishon. To drive the lesson home, she said, "Repeat after me, 'I will be abstinent.'"

"'I will be abstinent.' What's abstinence, Mom?"

"Abstinence is when you don't have sex."

"What's sex, Mom?"

"Well . . . you know . . . sex is like when you're hugging and kissing."

"Oh! I see, Mommy. You have sex every day. You're always hugging somebody!"

*   *   *

Teaching children to keep themselves sexually pure, to be abstinent, requires a holistic, multifaceted approach. It doesn't happen in one day, and it doesn't begin and end with one conversation. It is a process of cultivating essential life skills in children so that they are spiritually grounded, morally sound, and sexually pure.

Teaching kids to honor God and to express themselves appropriately and helping them to recognize their gifts and talents, for example, or teaching the value of self-control and helping them to recognize true friendships are ways parents teach the whole person. The goal is for children to develop into mature, balanced, secure, confident adults. What are the roads that lead to this end? What should we teach at every stage? (What follows is summarized in the charts on pages 76-79.)

Infants and Toddlers

Infants and toddlers are dependent on their parents for everything. This is the stage when parents lay a foundation of security and trust by meeting the child's needs by doing such things as cuddling, feeding, and diapering.[1] Since security is key, placing babies in the care of others too quickly may cause these little ones to experience feelings of abandonment. Mothers who are returning to work should not place their infants in day care too early. Even leaving young babies in the church nursery on Sunday mornings should be thought through. Eighteen months may be a good time to begin the separation process. And even then one parent should remain in the nursery until the infant is comfortable in this new environment.

The careful observer will affirm that children who are calm and confident are children who are parented by their mothers and fathers and/or primary caregivers such as grandparents. Financial pressures may force some married as well as single mothers to work outside the home and to have to place their youngsters in day care. Arguments abound that children raised in day care are well adjusted, but such reasoning flies in the face of common sense. If babies need to feel loved and secure, then every time they are left in the care of a stranger, they may feel a lack of love and security. Working part time and having a caregiver come to the home so that children remain in their own familiar environment might be a better alternative.

Routine is good. Developing schedules that are not rigid but consistent give young children a sense of order and organization.

At this age, children are discovering the world around them, and they are discovering their bodies too. It's normal for infants to touch themselves, but parents must help children learn what is appropriate and what is not. Parents should not overreact and attach adult motives to childish behavior.

When toddlers play with themselves, lectures and spankings are not generally in order. Distract them by giving them something else to do. Psychologists caution that overly sexual children may have been victims of abuse at some point, so be alert to behavior that seems to be excessive.

Ages Two and Three

At ages two and three, children are learning motor skills and are less dependent on adults. Each tiny activity, like learning new words or how to color, is a major accomplishment. Giving encouragement and applauding successes fill the educational process with joy.

When toddlers make mistakes—and they will—turn on the positives with encouragement like "Good try!" and "Try again!" Parents who affirm these efforts help build confidence. Children trust their own ability to be successful and are eager to try new ventures. These are part of a firm foundation, which is so essential for later years.

Ages Four, Five, and Six

As language and reading skills develop, children learn more about themselves and the world around them. Teaching them that certain areas of their body are "private" is the start of training them to be sexually pure. One parent explained this to her four-year-old.

* * *

"The part of your body that is in your underpants is the part of your body that you are not to show anyone. No one should see it except Mommy and Daddy, Grandma and Grandpa, or the doctor if Mommy and Daddy are with you.

"And no one is to touch you there. If anyone does, you must tell Mommy or Daddy. Don't let anyone tell you that it's a secret. There are good secrets and bad secrets. If anyone touches you there, that's a bad secret that you don't have to keep."

* * *

Some experts suggest teaching young children the correct names for their genitals. A parent who did soon realized how fascinated her four-year-old was with everyone's reaction whenever he said the word *penis*, so he said it all the time! Knowing your children and using common sense is perhaps the best rule of thumb.

Modeling modesty is wise. Parents should not bathe with their children, and as a habit, children should not sleep in the same bed with adults.

When children begin school, they may come home with many questions. Answer them simply, and don't read into the question, which is easy to do from an adult's perspective. Clarify new terms and words, and give explanations that are easy to understand. Children repeat what they hear other adults and other children say, so choosing schools carefully is a parent's first priority.

Teaching children values like honesty and respect for themselves and others helps build character. Bible stories are the place to begin, and there is an endless selection of storybooks for children that reinforce these traits.

Ages Seven, Eight, and Nine

Elementary school children need a lot of attention, support, and encouragement. Developing interpersonal skills and learning how to select friends, handle disagreements, and negotiate in different environments are challenges faced on a daily basis.

Here is where the foundation of communication is laid. Spend time talking with children around the dinner table, for example. Helping children resolve disputes and think through their problems are important aspects of building good relationships. Those who have experienced the loss of a parent through death, divorce, or separation especially need to share their feelings with someone they trust. The world isn't an ideal place, and unfortunately, many begin to learn this truth at too young an age.

Affirming children's feelings and reassuring them of God's love, care, and provision are assignments for the home. Yes, taking children to Sunday school or children's church is important, but it's only valuable when reinforced by consistent models in their everyday world. Adults teach love and forgiveness by apologizing to children when they make mistakes. Adults teach the value of honesty when their own children hear them tell the truth. And adults teach sexual purity when children see mothers and fathers who are committed to each other or single parents who have decided to live holy.

Teach children to stand up for their faith, and encourage them to share biblical truths even if Christians are a minority in their classes. Lessons about evolution are usually the place to begin. Of course, whenever possible, have your children attend schools that reinforce your values and Christian beliefs.

Ages Ten, Eleven, and Twelve

Not to be overlooked is the importance of sports and developing children artistically. Encourage kids to explore different interests after school hours and beyond school walls. Learning other languages and how to play an instrument are valuable life skills. Teaching patience, perseverance, understanding, and teamwork will help children become people who are fun to be around.

As much as possible, take kids on trips to explore the great outdoors. With television and the Internet taking over our lives, the effort to remain in touch with nature must be more intentional. Camps, retreats, and family times together help ease the normal stresses of daily living. Expand your children's world. Travel to a new state or even to a new country.

At this stage, children love to label one another and call names. We must teach them that this is *not* okay. Adults set the example by speaking to children with respect and by not calling their own children names. No matter how kids misbehave, we must remember that they are kids and we are adults, and adults must lead by example.

Now is a good time to begin the discussion about sexual purity. Explain what sexual intercourse is and that it is God's design for marriage. Tell kids the truth. Sex is wonderful, but it is for a special time—for married people only. Use every opportunity to educate about God's standards, and be alert to messages in our environment that violate God's laws.

Tell your children about the bodily changes they are going to experience *before* they happen so your preteens won't be caught off-guard. Since some children develop earlier than others, there is no set age to begin this dialogue, but talk with your children before their teachers or friends do.

Also discuss how differently they are going to *feel*. Hormones will awaken urges, and it is important to reassure preteens that these feelings are okay. That's how God designed us. The feelings themselves aren't bad, but we have to make the right decisions about what to do with those feelings. Self-control is a virtue to be exercised.

Puberty and the attendant feelings are enough to make any child feel insecure. Many feel awkward, and they are at this age, tripping, breaking dishes, and knocking things over. But calling children "clumsy" or making fun of their mistakes is nothing less than cruel.

Body image is a major concern during the preteen years. Children tend to feel too fat or too skinny. Either way, they should be reminded that how they look now is temporary. They will continue to grow and develop, and their bodies will continue to change.

Without good eating habits, excessive weight gain and a poor complexion become a preteen's worst nightmare. Good nutrition begins when we are very young, and using nutritional common sense should last a lifetime. Overweight children are likely to develop poor self-image—a danger sign that may signal early sexual involvement.

Parents who allow their children to be fat are irresponsible. Period. The lack of a balanced diet and consistent exercise are evident. It's worth it to make the effort to see an expert for help in getting the family's diet under control. Limit fast foods to no more than once a week, and commit to meals consisting mainly of fresh fruits and vegetables. Sugar, sweets, sodas, candy—the preferred menu of most kids—must be curbed. Shop and cook creatively so that your children don't end up hating their bodies and loathing the way they look.

Psychologists say that bluntly telling kids they're overweight has been known to cause eating disorders such as anorexia or bulimia. Calling children names such as "fat" or using other pejoratives (porky, tubby, etc.) under the guise of being playful is insensitive . . . and cruel. If children *are* eating balances meals, there may be a medical explanation for the excessive weight gain. Know your children, work with your doctor, and seek counsel.

Ages Thirteen, Fourteen, and Fifteen

At this age, kids are pressured to smoke, drink, and take drugs; and talking about this must begin long before these temptations are ever presented. Let your children know how you feel. They will listen.

Also, keep talking about the importance of abstinence and sexual purity. Let girls know the kinds of things boys may say to them, and teach boys how to handle pressure from girls and their peers.

How children dress and what they wear speak volumes about how they feel about themselves. Provocative clothing—clothes that are too tight, too short, too sheer, too skimpy—shouldn't be purchased. Give teens freedom to select their clothing, but shop with them and help them make decisions so they know what isn't acceptable. Since parents' wages buy the clothing, it is fitting for parents to participate in the decision making.

Teach girls to speak, sit, and walk properly. Learning the social graces, including how to conduct oneself in formal restaurants—for example, which forks to use and how to "pinch and butter" when eating bread—are all a part of maturing.

Ages Sixteen, Seventeen, and Eighteen

At this age, it's difficult for teens to remember they're not yet adults. As many parents can attest, young people often need as much supervision as do two-year-olds. For children of any age, there's nothing worse than being home alone.

I can't stress enough the importance of at least one parent being at home when their teens are at home. Several years ago, in a discussion with high school students on the program *Nightline*, television journalist Ted Koppel seemed shocked to hear kids say they were having sex right in their own homes—and sometimes in their parents' beds. They didn't have to hunt for hidden away places, because nothing was as convenient as having sex at home. Why? Their folks weren't there.

Experimentation is easy when adult supervision is absent. While parents are out earning a living and working hard to get ahead, they are often leaving behind the ones they care about most. Who can blame latch-key kids for making their own rules and doing what makes sense to them? Without the guidance and protection of those who know better, immature minds throw caution to the wind. And the breeze often blows right through our own homes!

Contrary to popular notions, most teens care deeply about how their parents feel. They value their opinions and want their approval. The role of parents doesn't decrease at this time. In fact, it is more important than ever. With so many decisions to make—from career choices to decisions about college or trade schools—teenagers need their mothers and fathers and cherish their participation in their lives.

To date or not to date is perhaps the biggest question during these years. While parents can't watch their children all the time, setting reasonable boundaries helps keep kids safe. Where are they going, and with whom? Monitoring your children's activities doesn't mean you don't trust your kids; it shows that you love them.

Dating is not a teenager's "right." Parents ultimately decide depending on the occasion and the kids, but, according to Dr. Laura Schlessinger, the popular family doctor, allowing dating for children who are younger than age seventeen is an invitation for trouble. Always set curfews and enforce consequences if curfews are broken. Ask questions and be very, *very* nosy. It's your job!

Help teens evaluate the reason they want to date. Many hold romantic notions and think that experience is essential for recognizing their future mate, but that isn't true. Talk about this with your kids. And also discuss the dangers of kissing and touching and toying with passions and emotions all for the sake of a little experience. Purity is more than just being a virgin. It's an attitude, the heart's desire to please God above all else.

Going out on a weekly basis should never be the norm. A teenager does not have the *right* to go out every weekend. That's asking for trouble. But if there are special events at school or at church, and if parents feel comfortable about the people and the plans, then they may consider giving their approval.

Once again, when kids are living at home, *parents* have the ultimate decision of saying yes or no. It's not about being liked by your kids, but be reasonable. It's about doing what's right for your kids. And what may be right for one child may be wrong for another. Know your own children, and guide them accordingly.

Books abound on the pros and cons of dating, and there are exciting discussions about the differences between courtship and dating. Parents and teens reading these books together may be better able to make wise decisions. And, as we'll see in the next chapter, parents don't have to be perfect to expect their children to remain pure.

What to know when	GOD THE FATHER, SON, AND HOLY SPIRIT	GOD-ESTEEM (also known as self-esteem)	THE BODY
5-6 years old	God created the world, created you, gives you life, protects you, and provides for you. He loves you, wants the best for you.	You are special, very special! You are part of God's family.	Your body is special! Each part of the body has a name. No one is to touch you in private areas except the doctor if your parent is present. There is a right way to play games such as "doctor," and a wrong way to play.
7-8 years old	God loves us. God is our Father. Jesus is his Son. Jesus sent the Holy Spirit to help us. The Bible is our guide. Prayer is talking to God. Jesus wants to be our best friend.	Respect yourself. Treat others with respect—in what you say, how you say it, and what you do. There are consequences for every decision we make, whether good or bad.	God designed you and has a special plan for your life. Ask Jesus Christ to be your Savior. God will give you wisdom to make right decisions about how to treat your body—proper grooming, what you eat.
9-10 years old	God created us for a purpose. We are to read and obey his Word. The Holy Spirit will help us.	Our friends are important, but we are important, too. Remember who you are: a child of God first and foremost.	God wants us to honor him with our lives. Honor begins with how we take care of the body. Treat it special, and treat others with respect, too, especially your parents (or caregivers).
11-12 years old	God expects us to obey him. We can do everything God tells us to do in his Word.	Our gifts and talents are from God. We are unique. Treat yourself with dignity. Dress with modesty. Our identity is in Jesus Christ.	Your body is changing, preparing you to be an adult. These changes are different for boys (wet dreams) and girls (menstruation). Other changes (height, voice, feelings) are natural, the way God made us. Some changes may feel awkward, and that's okay.

part 1 parents: the message begins at home

What to know when	EMOTIONS	WHAT IS APPROPRIATE	THE BIRTH PROCESS
5-6 years old	It's okay to cry. It's okay to be angry. But there are rules, and sometimes we may not like them. Still, we have to learn to be obedient, even if we don't feel like doing what is right.	There are good secrets, and there are "bad" secrets. If anyone touches you in a way that makes you feel uncomfortable, tell your parents. You don't have to keep a "bad" secret. Never lie to your parents!	Babies come from God. He designed that children should live in families with a mommy and a daddy.
7-8 years old	Feelings and emotions can let you know when something is wrong. If something happens that makes you feel bad, ask your parents for help.	You have the right to say no. No one, not even a teacher, can demand that you do anything about any private area of your body. Tell your parents. Don't let anyone show you any pictures or talk in ways that make you feel uncomfortable. If you have questions, ask your parents.	Babies come from the special union that God designed. This relationship is for husbands and wives only. The commitment of marriage is the true evidence of love.
9-10 years old	It is normal for boys to want to hang out with boys, and for girls to hang out with girls. This does not mean you are gay. Feelings of love do not have to lead to sex. And sex is not love.	Boundaries keep you safe. Friends have boundaries, too. Friendships can be appropriate or inappropriate. If you must sneak and lie to your parents, that is an inappropriate friendship.	Everything God made is good, including sexual intercourse — when a husband and a wife have sex (the penis enters the vagina). But there is a boundary for sex, and that boundary is marriage.
11-12 years old	Parents can't read your mind. It is important to tell them how you feel, even if they disagree. Holding onto feelings without expressing yourself can lead to destructive behavior. Think before you speak.	Do not participate in any school activity that tells you to disobey God's laws. You are a distinct person. Decide for yourself. Don't abuse your body with bad attitudes, drugs, alcohol, sexual intercourse, oral sex, or inappropriate touching.	Sin has consequences. These include sexually transmitted diseases such as HIV/AIDS. These illnesses can affect people the rest of their lives. When pregnancy occurs, we have children. When abortion is the decision, a baby is murdered, and the baby's parents are wounded emotionally.

at every stage chapter 5

What to know when	GOD THE FATHER, SON, AND HOLY SPIRIT	GOD-ESTEEM (Also known as self-esteem)	THE BODY
13-14 years old	God gives us laws so that we can live safe lives. The Holy Spirit gives us the ability to obey God and have self-control. When Jesus is our Savior, God wants us to allow the Holy Spirit to guide, direct, and control our lives. Fellowship with believers, study, pray, obey.	Respecting parents is evidence that we respect ourselves. No one (not teachers, not friends) is more important than God. What qualities distinguish a real friend from a false friend? How can we tell if a friend cares about us or is just using us? Remember, bad company corrupts good morals.	Your body is constantly changing. God designed it as his temple. You are fearfully and wonderfully made. How you look now is temporary. It is your attitude and actions, not looks, that determine who you really are. Honor your parents in the Lord.
15-16 years old	What is God's will for your life? What college should you attend? Pray and ask for his guidance, direction, and provision for every aspect of life. Measure your life by biblical standards. Read and study the Bible.	You are different because you are royal! You are a leader, not a follower. You may be the only one in your class who honors and obeys God, and that makes you very special. Always put God first. Evaluate your life—celebrate who you are. Evaluate friends: Which ones are true? Be selective! Love yourself first.	The body is God's temple. We have feelings, but they should not control what we do. Having feelings is okay and does not mean we are doing anything wrong. What we do with those feelings is what's important. Guard the mind, eyes, and ears, which affect how you feel.
17-18 years old	God is to be praised for all he has done. Apart from him, nothing of value and worth can be accomplished. We are his. Our life belongs to God.	Anyone who asks us to do anything that disobeys God is not a true friend. Put God first. We belong to him. We are special, and God has a special plan for us. We were born on purpose—God's purpose. The body is his temple. God lives in us.	Boundaries provided by God are to keep us safe. Boundaries keep good things in, bad things out. Crossing the line has consequences. Don't allow anyone to cross the boundary lines of the body. Oral sex and touching private parts lead to intercourse and are for husbands and wives only.

part 1 parents: the message begins at home

What to know when	EMOTIONS	WHAT IS APPROPRIATE	THE BIRTH PROCESS
13-14 years old	God makes us able to control thoughts and feelings. What we feed the mind determines how we think, and that determines how we feel. Our feelings are not "in charge." We are! Sexual intercourse is the strongest emotional bond between two people. There are consequences when we violate God's laws: hurt feelings, non-marital births, abortions.	There are different roles for men and for women, but different does not mean inferior or superior. Remember to guard your eyes, your ears, your mind. Be careful about television, the Internet, and the kind of music you listen to. You are precious and valuable, so take care of your body (grooming, etc.). Be wise!	Just because your body can make a baby doesn't mean that you are ready to be a parent. You are still developing mentally, physically, spiritually, emotionally. While some teens may think they are ready to have sexual intercourse, that does not mean you are. If there is a question, "How far is too far?" it is already too far. Commit to sexual purity, in thoughts and actions.
15-16 years old	How we feel sometimes dictates how we dress, especially girls in mid-cycle. The hormones make the body feel very sexy. Knowing this helps us keep the body in check. Never leave the house without checking yourself in a floor-length mirror. Remember, sexual intercourse will not boost a poor self-image.	Because life has purpose, we must protect our future. We can have self-control. We can decide in advance what we will and will not do — and stick to our decisions. Dating is not a right, but a privilege. Supervised group dating provides safe boundaries. If we find ourselves in a wrong situation, we can pray for a way of escape.	Biblical guidelines tell us how to be acceptable to God. There are spiritual, emotional, and physical consequences for everything we do. We do not have to behave the way people around us do; they may not know Jesus as Savior. Honor God. Recommit to sexual purity. Know what real love is and what it looks like. There is healing for victims of sexual abuse.
17-18 years old	Our bodies grow faster than our emotions develop. We may feel mature, but are not yet adults. Feelings of independence can be healthy. Being disobedient can make us feel "grown up," but are we? Feelings can and must be controlled. We have the God-given ability to live a pure, holy life.	Setting boundaries means we care about ourselves. Prom is not a time for sexual intercourse. Don't let anyone violate your boundaries. We deserve to be treated with respect. We show how important we are by what we do. Love is commitment, and commitment is marriage.	Being wise means thinking ahead and making decisions in advance. What kind of spouse meets your spiritual and emotional needs? What kind of spouse will you be? Keep yourself pure for your spouse. Sexual intercourse is for marriage only. Plan to marry someone who has also remained sexually pure. Sexually active teens can commit to secondary virginity and are just as pure in God's eyes.

at every stage chapter 5

chapter 6

but I'm not perfect

You shall not commit adultery.
Exodus 20:14

Sexual purity. Parents may feel disqualified in raising a standard they didn't maintain themselves. Because of disobedience in their own lives, they may hesitate to communicate the expectation that their children remain sexually pure. Some may feel that because of their history, they have no right to do so. They remain silent, believing that their children cannot be expected to do what they themselves didn't do. This is a lie from the pit of hell. Parents don't have to be perfect.

* * *

"I was so promiscuous, and I'm alive today only by the grace of God," one mother lamented. She was worrying about her eleven-year-old daughter, whom she wants to teach to be sexually pure. This mother feels inadequate because of her own lifestyle before she was married.

"My daughter must not make the same mistakes that I made. I don't know how to tell her, and I worry so much. Being sexually promiscuous today will kill her!"

Imperfect Perfection

They were the perfect parents. God the Father selected them to nurture, protect, and raise his Son, Jesus Christ. As perfect as they were, even they made mistakes.

The gospel writer Luke records an event that would strike terror into the hearts of any parent: Mary and Joseph lost the boy Jesus for three days!

When Jesus was twelve years old, the family traveled from Nazareth to Jerusalem for the Feast of the Passover, as was their annual custom (Luke 2:41-52). After the festivities, the family headed home. "Thinking he was in their company, they traveled on for a day. Then they began looking for him among their relatives and friends" (v. 44).

It is easy to imagine. Mary may have been traveling in a caravan with the women and thought that the boy was with his father, and Joseph may have been traveling with the men and assumed that the boy was with his mother. Perhaps at dinner they realized that neither of them had the child. Nor was he with any of their relatives or friends.

Frantic, they returned to Jerusalem (another day's journey), looking for Jesus at every step of the way. "Did you see Jesus? Have you seen our son? He was wearing. . . . He's this tall . . . . His hair is this color . . . . The last place we saw him was. . . ." They anxiously searched for him, but it took another entire day for them to find Jesus (v. 48).

Can you feel their panic? How could they have *lost* the Savior? How could they possibly forget Jesus?

Here were the ones whom the Father trusted, the most perfect parents in the world, and even they made a mistake. While their error was certainly not sexual in nature—Mary was a virgin at Jesus' birth—still we see a flaw that might have caused some of us to point the finger in sharp accusation.

When we view these parents through the eyes of grace, we can easily understand how such an event might have happened. It gives us pause to realize that even with the best intentions, there are times when parents are less than perfect.

Avoiding the Pitfalls

Protecting our children means helping them avoid the pitfalls that some of us may have plummeted into. Because we love our kids, we don't want them to experience sin's heartache, and we should tell them so. Obeying God and making right decisions will save them from sin's consequences.

The beauty of forgiveness is that the past is just that—the past. It is forgiven and forgotten. Guilt no longer has the right to raise its ugly head and accuse anyone. Christians are righteous, which means that we are in right standing with God because of faith in Jesus Christ. Righteous also means that we are right acting—*living right.*

No matter how much a parent's past may have reeked of sin, God no longer remembers it. It is forgiven. And that's that!

> Now one of the Pharisees invited Jesus to have dinner with him, so he went to the Pharisee's house and reclined at the table. When a woman who had lived a sinful life in that town learned that Jesus was eating at the Pharisee's house, she brought an alabaster jar of perfume, and as she stood behind him at his feet weeping, she began to wet his feet with her tears. Then she wiped them with her hair, kissed them and poured perfume on them.
>
> When the Pharisee who had invited him saw this, he said to himself, "If this man were a prophet, he would know who is touching him and what kind of woman she is—that she is a sinner."
>
> Jesus answered him, "Simon, I have something to tell you."
>
> "Tell me, teacher," he said.
>
> "Two men owed money to a certain moneylender. One owed him five hundred denarii, and the other fifty. Neither of them had the money to pay him back, so he canceled the debts of both. Now which of them will love him more?"
>
> Simon replied, "I suppose the one who had the bigger debt canceled."
>
> "You have judged correctly," Jesus said.
>
> Then he turned toward the woman and said to Simon, "Do you see this woman? I came into your house. You did not give me any water for my feet, but she wet my feet with her tears and wiped them with her hair. You did not give me a kiss, but this woman, from the time I entered, has not stopped kissing my feet. You did not put oil on my head, but she has poured perfume on my feet.
>
> Therefore, I tell you, her many sins have been forgiven—for she loved much. But he who has been forgiven little loves little."
>
> Then Jesus said to her, "Your sins are forgiven." The other guests began to say among themselves, "Who is this who even forgives sins?" Jesus said to the woman, "Your faith has saved you; go in peace."
>
> Luke 7:36-50

This woman's love was as deep as her sin, because Jesus reached just that deeply into her heart to heal and forgive her. Who wouldn't be overwhelmed with gratitude? While others judge, the Judge had declared righteous all who confess and repent—agree with God and turn from sin. The promise of 2 Corinthians 5:17 is especially for believers with a past. The old has gone, the new is come!

Our challenge is to remember that God's Word is true. He separates our sin from us as far as the east is from the west. Now, since God has forgiven us, shouldn't we forgive ourselves?

> The LORD is compassionate and gracious, slow to anger, abounding in love. He will not always accuse, nor will he harbor his anger forever; He does not treat us as our sins deserve or repay us according to our iniquities. For as high as the heavens are above the earth, so great is his love for those who fear him; as far as the east is from the west, so far has he removed our transgressions from us. As a father has compassion on his children, so the LORD has compassion on those who fear him.
>
> Psalm 103:8-13

God our Father does not ask us to do anything that he does not also give us the power to do through the Lord Jesus Christ who sent the Holy Spirit to help us. Everyone—whether divorced, single, separated, or married—can live sexually pure, because God gives the power to do so.

* * *

It was the morning of my wedding day. I had spent the night at the bed and breakfast where my husband-to-be and I would spend our first night together. *Today,* I thought as I watched the rain dance in the streets, *I am a bride!*

I had prayed for rain. California is all the more beautiful when the air is cleansed by a morning burst of showers. God had been faithful to answer my prayer for rain. And God's faithfulness was the banner of my heart. At the wedding, the soloist would sing, "Great is Thy Faithfulness," because God's Word had proven to be true in my life.

Ten years earlier I had committed myself to the Lord Jesus Christ. I had been saved as a child, but during my college years I pulled away from God. Logic became more important to me than Scripture. Astrology and the occult had more immediate answers.

Success propelled me to the height of a career in beauty, but every new accomplishment left me in the depths of despair. I felt empty still. No matter how hard I worked, it was not enough to fill the void.

"Have faith in God." My brother had preached this sermon the Sunday before. *I do, I do have faith in God*, I thought as I strained to see the words through the puddle of tears. Reading again, I seemed to hear the Lord say, "Have faith in *God's* ability. You have faith in your own ability."

It was true. A so-called self-made woman, I had tried to fashion myself into the image of decorum and finesse. I wanted to be what I had always admired, even though it contrasted so with the realities of my childhood. Our family life had been disrupted by separation and divorce, which either resulted from or caused my mother's mental illness. So troubled were the early years that it's hard to say which caused which.

The result, however, was distinguishable in the core of my personality, a fragile, raggedy self-esteem. To compensate, I had worked to be successful, only to find my life emptier still. I was constantly in a state of severe loneliness that felt like a giant hole in my heart. That day the Holy Spirit breathed hope into my hopelessness, and thinking it an idea of my own, I resolved to move from New York to Los Angeles for a fresh start.

The rain had stopped now. The sun emerged immediately and mingled with the rain to form a gentle crystal layer on the street below. I went to style my hair and realized that I had forgotten to pack my curling wand. *Nothing will ruin my wedding day.* I smiled at the thought and improvised. *I'm getting married today.*

I was a single mother raising my niece, soon to officially become my daughter, and a first-time bride at age forty-two. As a single woman with a child, and being over forty with the additional handicap of two degrees, statistics screamed that I would never marry. For a while I thought so, too, but God intervened.

When I arrived in Los Angeles, the world seemed wonderful again. There were new people to meet, a new church to join. The morning I entered the sanctuary, a woman who seemed younger than my then thirty-two years was the greeter at the door.

"Good morning and welcome to our church!" Joy burst from her heart, and I caught a whiff of the fruit of the Spirit's fragrance. Tears came to my eyes.

"Whatever she has, that's what I want," I said to myself as I entered the sanctuary. My decision to join the church was made right there with her greeting, even before I heard the pastor preach.

The church resounded with praise from young people who loved the Lord. I had never seen such a sight. They actually believed God's Word and were excited about him. I couldn't wait to walk down the aisle and recommit my life to Jesus Christ.

Wasting no time, the Lord began to dismantle my carefully orchestrated junk. The first thing to go was astrology. Mine was not the casual involvement of those who read newspaper horoscopes. I had three personal astrologers whom I paid and upon whom I relied. Their predictions were close, but there was always an unknown twist with a tinge of disappointment. Still, having partial answers about the future was enough to soothe my childhood uncertainties and protect me from the onslaught of surprise. The second sermon I heard in my new church scared me straight. The message explained that astrology is idolatry and that relying on the stars is an abomination to God (Deut. 18:9-14).

That morning, three minutes into the message, I was so frightened I could hardly breathe. Was I courting demons? I confessed to the pastor afterward and hurried home to burn all my astrology books. The next Sunday I asked to recite during the evening service this poem I had penned in the light of newfound faith.

My Sign? The Cross!

When I am at a loss about the future
And wonder what sweet promise tomorrow brings
The stars are not where I look to find an answer
Through prayer I turn to Christ who knows all things

You ask where is my sun? What sign my rising?
Or where my moon at birth by chance may be?
I've burned all trust (Praise God!) in earthly matters
The only sign I need is Calvary.

I don't marvel at the planets in their orbit,
No longer chart the movement of the stars
I look past these to the throne of my heavenly Father
To Christ, the King of Kings and Lord of Lords

He alone holds my todays, plans my tomorrows
He alone decides what path I am to take
All I need do is yield my will completely
And let the Potter good of this vessel make

Oh how simple now it seems this revelation!
Oh how pure and true the hope this faith can bring!
The only sign I need for life's direction
Is trust in God above for everything

My sign? The Cross! The Cross, my sign!
What joy rings in my heart this blessed day
I see the heavens as God's for just His glory
The precious Holy Spirit leads my way

Step by step, step by step, Dear Lord, guide me
Teach me to walk by faith and not by sight
With my hand in Thine, one day at a time, Lord purge me
That I might help bring others to Your Light

November 9, 1980

Clothed in a New Gown

I was now totally dependent on God. Although I thought I knew the Scriptures, I devoured the Bible like a newborn babe. There was life in this Book! Prayer was my passport throughout each day. Now, having no astrological answers, each step of each day was truly a walk of faith.

As I read God's Word, it spotlighted my sexual sin with warnings I had always assumed were surely only meant for unbelievers. Fornication? That's how the unsaved behaved. While in college during the sexual revolution of the late sixties, we rationalized that we were "making love." During this time, I was in a constant struggle to find myself—an admission that I would make almost daily. My stepmother would then ask me, "But when were you lost?"

I went to church all the time. My dad was the pastor, so I was very, very busy working as superintendent of the Sunday school, as a member of the pastor's aid, and even as a member of the choir. Unfortunately, that was the extent of my commitment. I was in the church, but the church was not in me.

Relying on Sunday morning messages to get me through the week, I did not read or study the Bible for myself on a regular basis. The consequence was acute spiritual malnutrition couched in a wounded personality that stemmed from a troubled childhood. My birth mother could not handle the stress of raising children, and she often resorted to physical abuse.

With damaged self-esteem, I thought of myself as garbage, an impression that persisted in spite of my dad's remarriage, my graduation from a private Christian high school, and my acceptance into a prestigious college.

Wanting more than anything else in the world to be accepted by my peers as a freshman, I cringed whenever they teased me because I was still a virgin. Not realizing that misery loves company, by my sophomore year I was determined to shed this label so that I could fit in with the crowd. Little did I know the price

I would pay emotionally. Finally, though, I belonged. The definitions of who I was came from the people around me. Inside, I felt like a hollow mess.

To mask the feelings of inadequacy, I worked hard at a magazine career and became quite successful. In 1979 I landed a book contract and wrote my first beauty book. Finally, I was a real success and began to freelance as a writer for many of the leading women's magazines. Everything was perfect—except that inside, I still felt as if I had a gaping hole that needed to be stuffed with love. Moving 3,000 miles away from everything familiar, I at last found the acceptance I needed in God's Word: "If you love Me, you will keep My commandments" (John 14:15 NASB).

I realized that if I did not keep God's commandments, it was because I really didn't love him. Now, like the woman with the alabaster box of perfume, I became acutely aware of my sin. With each verse I realized that simply going to church was not the measure of my love for the Lord but rather, it was how I lived my life when I was not in church.

It honestly didn't make sense to me that God could expect me to be sexually pure. The music I listened to, the television I watched, my conversations with my friends—these were the standards by which I lived.

In sheer desperation to stop the ache inside my heart, I fell to my knees one night and asked God to take over my life completely. I prayed this prayer: "I agree with you that what you call sin is sin. I give you permission to take over my life and make me the person you want me to be."

It was simple and short, but it seemed that evil spirits lifted from my shoulders. I literally felt physically lighter. And I determined to live holy, one day at a time.

As I memorized Scriptures by placing them on 3x5 cards around my apartment, I realized that many of the thoughts I believed were lies. How could I be lonely if Jesus said, "I will never, never leave you" (see Hebrews 13:5)? I shut off that recording in my mind that constantly repeated, "I'm so lonely."

Romans 12:1-2 became my cornerstone. I decided to put God to the test. If I presented my life to God, then I could expect to see his perfect will for my life. Since he was up to the challenge, so was I.

I applied the balm of Scripture to my heart. Rather than just hearing God's Word, I began applying, living, and obeying him completely. I didn't want to be with those who are described in Revelation 22 as being outside the gates of heaven.

Expecting the Scriptures to specify that believers would be inside the gate and unbelievers outside the gate, I was shocked to see that the lines of demarcation were defined by behavior. "Blessed are they that do his commandments" (Rev. 22:14 KJV). I realized that how I behaved was the truest measure of what I believed. Even the demons believe and tremble (James 2:19), but their belief does not change their behavior.

Scripture ruptured my abscessed personality and reshaped my raggedy self-esteem. I wanted to be married, but thought that because of my own childhood, I hated children. How could I possibly want a family?

God totally healed my memories the day that I sat on my couch and told him all about my life. Even though these were facts he already knew, I wanted to tell him again out loud. As I talked, I cried and said, "I forgive my mother by an act of my will." Soon I fell asleep. When I woke up, I knew that something was different.

Something *was* different. *I* was different. Several weeks later, I was offered a job to work in an elementary school, and to my amazement, I loved every moment. My ministry became that of speaking life and hope into the lives of children. And the ultimate joy of my life was raising my niece and adopting her as my daughter.

I defined myself in biblical terms. The words *precious, royal,* and *holy* were beautiful word pictures by which I colored a new me.

Irving and I met at a Christian retreat. There were no sparks or bells or whistles at first, no love at first sight. All I thought was that he would be a very good friend. On our third date, however, I had such a nervous stomach that I couldn't finish my dinner. On the fourth date, he proposed. He took me shopping for a ring later that week.

Today is my wedding day! I understood the value of sexual purity. I discovered my God-esteem and knew who I am in Christ. I knew how I deserved to be treated, and I understood that I am a jewel in the sight of God. He cleansed me, purified me, changed my mind . . . gave me a new mind. I'm transformed!

My daughter will have a father. Our family will be complete. I put on my white gown. *God is faithful.* My gown was sparkling like the sun-kissed raindrops. I put on my veil. *God's Word is true. His will is perfect.* The tulle graced my shoulders and made me look twenty years young.

Today, I'm a bride, giving myself to my husband with all of the passion of the Song of Solomon. We will be lovers. It will be holy. God himself will smile on us. I am my beloved's, and my beloved is mine. Our love is pure!

I hummed:

Amazing grace how sweet the sound that saved a wretch like me.
I once was lost but now am found, was blind but now I see!

Turning Around

When Jesus encountered the woman at the well (John 4), he turned her life around. She obviously knew all about religious ritual. But she knew nothing of redeeming relationship. Looking into the face of Jesus, she finally saw her true reflection. How refreshing to realize that he knew her, *really* knew her, yet loved her still. Perhaps that is why she abandoned her water jar—a symbol of her former way of life?—and ran throughout the city sharing her testimony.

The key for keeping one's children sexually pure is to keep oneself pure. Following are nine steps to freedom from sexual sin.

1. Agree with God that what he calls sin is sin.
2. Admit to God that your lifestyle is sin and that it violates his Word.
3. Acknowledge that you are powerless to stop your behavior.
4. Admit that you may not even want to change your behavior.
5. Allow God to clean up your life by the power of the Holy Spirit by giving him permission to do whatever he has to do to stop your lifestyle of sinning.
6. Accept God's chastisement and know that you are a child whom he loves.
7. Accept his forgiveness and cleansing and refuse feelings of guilt and condemnation.
8. Appropriate God's Word, to help you when tempted, by memorizing Scripture, repeating it often, and doing what the Bible says.
9. Accountability, either to a small group or to one or two friends you can trust provides a safe place of sharing, prayer, and repentance.

All of these steps are about *repenting*—that is, turning around and going in the opposite direction, for that is what the word means. Specifically, it means to turn away from sin and go in the direction of Jesus Christ.

Being sorry is not repenting; it is merely being sorry. The person who is sorry, even very, very sorry, will continue to sin. The apostle John writes:

> Dear children, do not let anyone lead you astray. He who does what is right is righteous, just as he is righteous. He who does what is sinful is of the devil, because the devil has been sinning from the beginning. The reason the Son of God appeared was to destroy the devil's work. No one who is born of God will continue to sin, because God's seed remains in him; he cannot go on sinning, because he has been born of God. This is how we know who the children of God are and who the children of the devil are: Anyone who does not do what is right is not a child of God.
>
> 1 John 3:7-10

A repentant heart is evident in a change of behavior. And with repentance comes this promise:

> If we confess our sins, he is faithful and just and will forgive us our sins and purify us from all unrighteousness.
>
> 1 John 1:9

A New Mind

A change in behavior results from a change of mind as well as a repentant heart. Romans 12:1-2 tells us to offer our bodies as living sacrifices, holy and pleasing to God, and not to conform to the pattern of this world, but to be transformed by the renewing of our minds. The mind is like a tape recorder. Messages are imprinted, and when they play, we react. We need to input new information to elicit new responses.

Studying God's Word is essential to holy living. And study involves more than just reading; it involves memorizing Scripture as well. If we hide Scripture in our hearts and minds, the Holy Spirit will bring the Word back to us in times of temptation. But how can one recall what has never been studied? The psalmist wrote,

> I have hidden your word in my heart, that I might not sin against you.
>
> Psalm 119:11

Filling our hearts and minds with trash, like music, movies, and television loaded with acts of sexual sin and disobedience to God is not wise. It's not that listening to secular music or watching television or going to the movies in and of themselves is sin. But we must make decisions about what our eyes will see, ears will hear, and minds will remember. The old data needs to be replaced with new data. After all, if garbage goes in, garbage will come out.

> The statues of the LORD are right, rejoicing the heart;
> The commandment of the LORD is pure, enlightening the eyes;
> The fear of the LORD is clean, enduring forever;
> The judgments of the LORD are true and righteous altogether.
> More to be desired are they than gold,
> Yea, than much fine gold;
> Sweeter also than honey and the honeycomb.
>
> Psalm 19:8-10 NKJV

Present versus Surrender

We can't live the Christian life in our own strength. We need to present, or give, our lives to God so that he can live through us. Often we sing, "I surrender all," to communicate that we give up. But a professor once explained that the term *surrender* is not biblical, because as in war, to surrender is to do something against one's will. The soldier with no other option is defeated and forced to be a prisoner of war. God does not want an army of unwilling prisoners.

The Bible tells us rather to *present* ourselves to God (Rom. 12:1), to willingly give our lives to the Savior. When we present ourselves we acknowledge that Christ in us lives his life through us. Victory is assured when at each sunrise we present ourselves anew and live holy one day at a time.

part 2

public schools:
the weakest link

"Why should I forgive you?
Your children have forsaken me
and sworn by gods that are not gods.
I supplied all their needs,
yet they committed adultery
and thronged to the house of prostitutes.
They are well-fed, lusty stallions,
each neighing for another man's wife.
Should I not punish them for this?"
declares the LORD.
"Should I not avenge myself
on such a nation as this?"
Jeremiah 5:7–9

It was my daughter's first day in junior high. After we checked in at the principal's office, I helped La Nej find her locker. She was eager for me to leave and kept assuring me that she'd be all right.

Since I was a single parent, private education was out of the question financially. To attend the public school of our choice, we had to move. Our new apartment was much smaller than the last, but it was also much more affordable. We only had a weekend to get settled before school began on Monday.

The halls seemed so large, and my child looked dwarfed by the other students. I didn't want to leave her, but without any good reason to hang around longer, I gave her a kiss and prayed that God would take care of her.

At home I read all the forms I was supposed to sign. When I reviewed the health forms, I knew that I was in for a fight. In no way was I permitting my daughter to sit in on any of their sex education classes.

chapter 7

what they're learning in sex ed

I hear a cry as of a woman in labor,
a groan as of one bearing her first child—
the cry of the Daughter of Zion gasping for breath,
stretching out her hands and saying,
"Alas! I am fainting;
my life is given over to murderers."
Jeremiah 4:31

Public schools today have become social service institutions focusing on the national agenda of providing comprehensive sex education and reproductive health care services to students. Often children are exposed to explicit sex education, given condoms and other contraceptives, and provided with birth control and abortions—all without parental notification or consent.

* * *

I graduated from New York's Hunter College in the fall of 1970. In 1975 my professional career as a magazine writer was solidly under way, and I had become active in community affairs. As a result, I was asked to join the board of Planned Parenthood, where I volunteered until 1980.

As a pastor's daughter raised in the church, I knew little about abortion. But I did believe—and debated in the college cafeteria—that every woman had a "right to choose." When abortion became legal in 1973, the consensus was that a certain freedom had finally been granted to women. Yet how many of us really knew exactly how abortions were performed?

My journey to the board of Planned Parenthood began with my involvement in a group called the Coalition of 100 Black Women, a New York City-launched socially conscious organization composed of businesswomen, politicians, and civic leaders. They wanted to empower a young voice, and although I was among the less exposed and less experienced, they voted to send me as their delegate to the first International Women's Year conference held in Mexico City in 1975. When a speech I made received media coverage back home, I was greeted with my organization's applause along with invitations to join two boards—the Young Women's Christian Association (YWCA) and Planned Parenthood.

I attended my first board meeting filled with anticipation. It was quite a short bus ride from the midtown office where I worked as an editor over to the Margaret Sanger Clinic, named after Planned Parenthood's founder. Over time I noticed that several of the board members arrived in chauffeured limousines. Who were these men of wealth, I wondered, and why were they so interested in the people who lived in the inner-city?

Once in the building, I walked past the clinic that served primarily African-American and Latino girls. The elevator took me upstairs to an imposingly large boardroom, and I took my seat with the striking observation that I was the only person of color in the room. The majority of board members were male, and the handful of women appeared to be much older than my twenty-seven years.

During the course of my five-year tenure, we received a lot of literature. Most discussed population control and the concern for the growing number of people in the world—poor people in the United States and in developing countries. As the population grew, natural resources like air, water, and food were shrinking. I soon understood why the full name for this organization was Planned Parenthood World Population.

I struggled with the question, "Which population are they trying to control?" As a black woman, the question kept coming back to me like a boomerang. I wondered why abortion was more necessary for my ethnic group, why this organization fought so hard to give *us* this particular "right" when the rights for better education, better jobs, and better housing seemed paramount.

Early in my volunteer service on the board, I learned about the biggest challenge that Planned Parenthood of New York City faced. For every abortion that was performed, a death certificate had to be issued by the Department of Health. They wanted to reverse this law.

Death certificates? Does that mean the babies were *alive?* Like millions of other Americans, I debated about when life really begins. When is the fetus viable? When can it live on its own? Abortion could not be murder if, indeed, all that was aborted was a "mass of tissue."

Part of our responsibility as board members was to become familiar with abortion procedures. We read documents detailing how abortions were performed, and for me, that's when the viability debate ended. I learned of two kinds of abortions—saline and dilation and evacuation, also called D & E. I would later learn about a third type, late-term or partial-birth abortion.

In saline abortions, babies inhale a salt solution that is introduced into the womb. The mother experiences premature labor and delivers a dead, burned baby. In instances where the baby is born still breathing, he or she is placed into a plastic bag, which is then sealed, and the baby is suffocated.

The dilation-and-evacuation abortion literally tears the baby apart limb by limb. The instrument used, insanely called a "straw," is actually a powerful suction device. It is inserted into the mother's uterus, where it searches for an arm or leg of the baby. Once it latches on, it tears that limb from the baby's body. Each limb is subsequently torn apart and suctioned, or "evacuated." Since the head is too large to pass through the nozzle of the "straw," the doctor has to insert an instrument that looks much like a clamp. It grasps the baby's head and crushes it into smaller pieces, which are then evacuated. A nurse puts all the pieces of the baby onto a nearby table, reassembling the body to make certain that all parts have been successfully removed from the uterus.

I was horrified. I came to the next meeting shaking with disbelief and filled with protestations. Holding up the papers, I said that these procedures were traumatic for both the mother and her baby.

An older woman sitting directly across from me looked me coldly in the eye and said in a low, rabid voice, "It is *not* traumatic!" I was stunned by her insensitivity and chilled by her icy stare.

I was on the verge of resigning from the board. Now that I understood what was really involved, I wanted no part in this abortion business. But the question, "Who will speak up if I leave?" kept me in a quandary. Eventually deciding to remain, I determined to be a thorn in their side and often cast the lone opposing vote.

The year that the chairman of the board, Al Moran, gleefully announced that thousands of abortions had been performed in New York State alone, shivers ran down my spine. When I slept that night, I had nightmares. I saw dead babies suspended between heaven and earth, floating motionless in a vacuous sky. I awoke with the horrifying knowledge that God would hold me accountable. We weren't just a board of directors. We were death's directors! I had to do something.

Planned Parenthood's Speaker's Bureau provided me opportunity for a more active role. I became a trained volunteer and my goal was to educate junior high and high school students before they ended up on an abortionist's table. The talk I developed was called "Love Carefully" (the slogan adopted from one of Planned Parenthood's short-lived campaigns), and it had a "Say No!" message. First, however, I had to complete Planned Parenthood's training. It was thorough and an eye-opener, revealing the subtle yet powerful use of language.

In the training sessions we were told never to use the words *embryo* (human offspring in the first eight weeks from conception) or *fetus* (human embryo more than eight weeks from conception). I later learned that *fetus* stems from a Latin word that means "little one." We were instead to use the inanimate terms "mass of tissue" or "contents of the uterus."

Language for addressing teen parents was also strategic. We were never to call a teenage girl a "mother." We were to refer to her as a "woman" no matter how young she might be. A teenage boy was never to be called a "father." He was to be called a "man."

I avoided discussing abortions in my talks at schools but was told that I had to explain and demonstrate the birth-control and contraceptive methods or else the schools would not permit me to give my talk. At the time I believed this was the schools' requirement and not Planned Parenthood's. To teenage boys and girls I had to explain the following.

Devices such as the intrauterine device (IUD) are birth control because they *control the birth* of a child. With the IUD, conception still occurs. The sperm fertilizes the egg, but the "woman" has a spontaneous abortion every month due to the presence of a foreign body—the IUD—in her uterus. Menstruation is usually heavy accompanied by severe cramps. Contraceptive devices (*contra* = "against" conception) are methods that prevent the sperm from meeting the egg: pill, diaphragm, foam, and condom.

Students were to be assured that parental notification or consent was not required for any of Planned Parenthood's services. If the "woman" visited a Planned Parenthood facility, she was to give the counselor the name of a friend who typically phoned her at home. Should a parent answer the telephone, the counselor would then use this girlfriend's name when she called to confirm an appointment.

Once in the classroom, these students were mine for two entire class periods. Sometimes several classes would be grouped together to hear my lecture. For most, it was the first time they had a conversation with an adult about sex, so I never had to ask students to be quiet or to pay attention. They knew we were talking about their bodies, their lives. And here was my chance to make a difference.

"What are your career goals? What do you want to be when you grow up?" I would ask. Helping kids set goals for their future provided the backdrop for my lecture. Listed on the board would be an array of careers from firefighter to beautician to doctor. "How are you going to get there?" I questioned. The answers included trade school, college, and so on. The next question transitioned to the point of the lecture.

"What could possibly interrupt your plans for the future?" The answer "becoming a mother or father" launched the discussion about ways to prevent a pregnancy from happening, beginning with what they had heard their friends say about how not to become pregnant.

Armed with chalk to write responses on the board, I would ask, "Tell me what you've heard your friends say." Some of their answers went like this:

> You can't get pregnant if you don't love him.
> You can't get pregnant if he doesn't love you.
> You can't get pregnant if it's your first time.
> You can't get pregnant if it's his first time.
> You can't get pregnant if you're standing up.
> You can't get pregnant if you don't enjoy it.
> You can't get pregnant if you don't have a climax.
> You can't get pregnant if you don't go all the way.
> You can't get pregnant if you've never had a period.
> You can't get pregnant if you're menstruating.
> You can't get pregnant if you don't want to.

With this list I would begin to explain how conception occurs or, as I put it, how the "sperm meets the egg." The depiction of the egg-shaped sperm with a wiggly tail helped to demonstrate how thousands of sperm swim upward at one time, each hoping to be the lucky one to find that egg.

"Does the sperm know whether or not you're in love? Does the egg care if it feels good?" Laughing and totally engaged, the answers were always "no." Next I would solicit ways that girls and boys pressure one another to have sexual intercourse.

> "If you loved me, you would."
> "I'm going to leave you if you don't."
> "This will bring us closer together."
> "We'll get married."

As we reviewed these pressure tactics, I also asked the students how they might respond. One of the wittiest retorts went like this. "No? What are you, a *nun?*" "Yeah! *None* for you!" Then I would ask the key question. "What's the best way to keep the sperm from meeting the egg?" Without fail, "Say no!" was the response. They were convinced!

Then, to comply with the policy, I would open my huge plastic bag of birth-control and contraceptive devices and explain how each worked. As I did so, I could see eyes widening and students leaning forward in their seats, their interest mounting. The impact of two hours of dialogue was swept away with the simple display of a condom or IUD.

"But what's the *best* way to keep the sperm from meeting the egg?" I would call out as students rushed to the table to see these devices up close. The "Say No" response always seemed pretty weak at that point.

I added to my "Love Carefully" talk descriptions of venereal diseases (VDs), as they were called in the 1970s. That was before the term changed to the more sophisticated "sexually transmitted diseases" (STDs) and the still less offensive "sexually transmitted infections" (STIs). Graphic explanations accompanied by pictures of genital warts, herpes, syphilis, and gonorrhea, and followed by the truth that birth control and contraceptives offered little protection against these diseases, was sobering to the students. I learned to counter their enthusiasm with the devices by ending with this discussion. Still, I knew I was giving two messages, and the two messages were conflicting and confusing.

Meanwhile, my career in magazine publishing was progressing nicely, and my first beauty book was published in 1979.[1] I accepted an offer to consult to a major cosmetic company and after a year of traveling decided to relocate from New York to Los Angeles.

I resigned from Planned Parenthood's board, but the burden of what I had learned and experienced followed me on my 3,000-mile move. One morning in my new apartment, I was overwhelmed with the need to pray for our nation. I lay prone on the floor. Through sobs, I asked God to forgive us and to somehow turn things around. When I got up and dried my face, I felt an inner resolve—a determination to do something, although I was not quite certain what that might be.

First, I realized I needed to research more about Planned Parenthood and its founder. One book in particular, *Grand Illusions: The Legacy of Planned Parenthood* by George Grant,[2] confirmed what I had experienced and taught me much, much more. In it I learned about the Negro Project, which was Margaret Sanger's directive that Planned Parenthood target African-American pastors. It dawned on me how valuable they considered me to be since I was a pastor's kid!

In this same book I learned of an organization called Black Americans for Life located in Washington, D.C. I contacted them, only to find they were no longer active. However, I was given the name of a black women closer to home—Janet Hudspeth. Black Californians for Life was birthed in 1991 with a handful of members. Janet served as Executive Director; Joyce Ashley and Blanche Cook were the dynamo team who initially educated me, and our community, about the dangers of school-based clinics; Carolyn Walker did extensive research on the life of Margaret Sanger; Dr. Minnie Claiborne was an expert who lectured on post-abortion syndrome; and Akua Furlow spearheaded efforts to start Black Californians for Life chapters in Texas. I was elected president.

Our goal, like Sanger's, was to target pastors, but of course, our objectives differed. We purposed to inform, educate, and expose the Black church to the truth about abortion through seminars, walks for life, and pastors' luncheons networking with Right to Life and Hispanics for Life. For the most part, however, Planned Parenthood had made such an inroad into the Black community that most pastors eyed us with disbelief. The exception was Pastor Edward Robinson who, after attending one of our workshops, opened a Crisis Pregnancy Center (CPC) in the heart of Compton in 1993 with Joyce's hands-on assistance. To date, this CPC has helped over 2,000 women.

In my role as president, I was often invited to speak. My talk was titled, "Planned Parenthood Is *Not* Your Friend." During one session, someone in the audience asked me whether or not death certificates were still required in New York when an abortion was performed. I decided to call the New York Department of Health to find the answer.

The department's Information Medical Division gave me this response: "A death certificate is not given unless the induced abortion is a live birth," no matter the gestation period as long as it is within a legal abortion time.

"What is considered to be a 'live birth'?" I asked.

"A birth is considered live if there is voluntary muscle movement or beating of the heart."

I probed even further. "By voluntary muscle movement, do you mean breathing?"

"Yes. The abortion is considered to be a live birth only if the baby takes a breath before it dies."

Only if it takes a breath . . .

In 1991, our attention focused on preventing RU-486, the pill that induces abortion, from being tested on women in California. A July 9th hearing was held at the Los Angeles County Board of Supervisors, and among the speakers faced with protecting the rights of the innocent poor were Susan Carpenter-McMillan, media spokesperson for Right to Life, Dr. Bernard Nathanson, cofounder of the National Abortion Rights Action League (NARAL), a young woman named Gianna Jessen, a saline-abortion survivor, and me.

The environment was volatile and hostile thanks to the taunting, shouts, and jeers of the homosexual activist group, Act Up, who were there to distract and intimidate us. The supervisors seemed unsympathetic, and to me, our efforts felt like a losing battle. There we were, little Davids, trying to make a giant—Planned Parenthood—fall.

When we were told how little time we each had to address the supervisors, I decided that rather than reading a prepared statement, I would look into their eyes and speak from my heart, nerves and all. I did, but were it not for Gianna's biography written by Jessica Shaver, I would scarcely remember what I said.

"I am saddened—in fact, last night I could not sleep—that RU486 has come this far. Black women comprise only 12 percent of the population, yet over half of those women undergo abortions. Minority women are the target of the abortion movement because we are the majority of the poor. If we do not stand up against RU-486, we are going to be the victims."[3]

I wanted to tell them about Faye Wattleton, the African-American president of Planned Parenthood who worked diligently to have an abortion pill in the United States. I wanted to tell them that during her presidency, Faye had been so successful because she only debated white men, preferably priests who wore clergy collars. And I wanted to alert them to the strategy of misleading sympathetic rhetoric that poor women especially needed family planning services, when poor women were unwittingly the targets. So much to say, so little time.

Despite our best efforts, including Gianna's emotional testimony about how she survived her mother's efforts to abort her and was born alive with cerebral palsy, the motion passed four to one. RU-486 would be tested on minority women in California after all. Goliath was still standing.

There were more stones to be uncovered, so my research continued. What I discovered next from a nurse who worked in abortion rooms was the most shocking and personally unbelievable information I had ever heard. It was about partial-birth or late-term abortions, which are still legal in this land of the free and home of the brave.

This abortion is performed by prematurely inducing the mother's labor. As the baby emerges, the doctor turns the child so that he or she is born breech—buttocks and feet first. As the baby's head is just about to emerge, an instrument is inserted into a soft place at the back of the skull, and the baby's brains are suctioned. This is done while the baby's head is still partially inside the mother's uterus so that the procedure is still technically an abortion and not infanticide. But does the fact that the baby's head has not fully emerged make the procedure anything less than infanticide? And isn't this barbaric? A late-term abortion can be performed up to the day that the baby is due.

I continued my research in the field beginning with the word *abortion*, which comes from the Latin *aboriri*. The root, *orior*, means "to be born" or "to rise" and connotes a process or regular phenomenon that occurs as a normal part of nature. An example of this kind of nature is the daily rising of the sun. As the day dawns, the sun rises and progresses in its motion until nightfall. At dusk we can expect the sun to continue in its natural course until it sets. Every day the sun rises, and every evening the sun sets. It is nature in motion, and it is impossible to prevent.

The prefix *ab* means "from" or "away" or "bringing to an end." *Ab* is used in front of words such as *abnormal* and *abandon*. When placed in front of the root *oriri*, we get the English word *abortion*, which connotes keeping a natural event—a birth—from occurring. *Abortion* means "to terminate prematurely" or, for the baby, "to perish by untimely death." Implied in the word *abortion* is the idea that the cessation of a birth is as unnatural as interfering with the rising of the sun.

Too often when a pregnant teen enters a clinic seeking help, abortion is the only option presented to her. She is told that she cannot afford to have a baby. She is presented with a summary of costs and asked if she has the money to meet these expenses. Encouraged that abortion is a quick, easy solution to her problem, she is assured that the "blob," "wart," "cyst," or "mass of tissue" is easy to remove. She is not shown the developmental stage of her baby, and she is not informed that her baby's heart is already beating or that her baby is already sucking its thumb. She is not warned of the emotional or physical side effects of the abortion. Nor is adoption presented as an alternative.

"Counselors" also tell girls that they can "tie their tubes" so they won't ever have to worry about becoming pregnant again. Since things like shoes can be tied and easily untied, the permanency of having one's tubes tied, or sterilization, may not register in a teenager's immature mind. However, girls may legally consent to sterilization without a parent's knowledge or consent. Teenage boys can also be sterilized without parental notification or consent.

My study continued with a background check of Planned Parenthood's founder, Margaret Sanger. Her autobiography sits on the shelf of most public libraries.[4] Sanger's eugenics philosophy, sharpened by her "socialist friends, lovers, and comrades [who] were committed eugenicists as well,"[5] is clearly stated: the improvement of the race through controlled breeding. Certain ethnic groups are categorically labeled as "dysgenic," meaning that they are biologically defective or deficient. These ethnic groups she called the "weeds" of society, and she was determined to "stop the multiplication of the unfit . . . [for] race betterment." Only certain groups should have the privilege of reproducing themselves, and this would guarantee "a cleaner race."[6]

Sanger was not a believer in abortion initially. She championed birth-control.[7] "Birth-control," said Sanger in 1920, "is nothing more or less than the facilitation of the process of weeding out the unfit, or preventing the birth of defectives, or of those who will become defectives."[8] I was astounded. Certainly this could not be the same woman who has been lauded and applauded by black women's magazines and groups as a symbol of women's rights?

In 1939 Sanger initiated the Negro Project.[9] The proposal called for selecting a Negro Steering Committee with candidates from Howard University. They should appear to run the campaign to squelch any thoughts of extermination. "We do not want the word to get out that we want to exterminate the Negro population, and the minister is the man who can straighten out that idea if it ever occurs to any of their more rebellious members."[10] Sanger realized the importance of the "colored minister" in his community and considered him to be of more value than any physician. Yet she considered religion to be an exercise in superstition, saying, "They still believe—large numbers of them—that God sends them children."[11]

I now understood more about the philosophical roots of the woman and the organization she launched. But for now, how Planned Parenthood became engrained in our nation's schools would remain a puzzle. The pieces would finally fit together years later during my dissertation research, which is discussed in the next chapter.

Armed with this information, it was easy to be passionate when speaking at conventions, conferences, or churches. But, I had to remember that in that same room, there undoubtedly were women who themselves had experienced the trauma of abortion. For the first time they might be learning the truth, and they might be sitting there filled with horror, remorse, and regret. I knew that these women, ignorant of the reality of their decision, were as much victims as were their babies, and a heavy dose of compassion had to be mingled with the facts.

Even now I realize that some readers might likewise feel shaken by what they have read. I don't want to be insensitive or continue with this book without pausing and acknowledging their pain and grief. I trust that the following true account from a woman who is now married and serving in the ministry full-time will encourage anyone who needs a healing touch from God.

* * *

"In 1985, at the age of twenty, I was involved in a sexual relationship with my first boyfriend, who was then, of course, the love of my life until I told him I was pregnant. I was shocked, confused, and filled with disbelief at the reaction of this man who professed his love for me and begged me to surrender my virginity to him. He turned his back on me, and the pregnancy became for me a not-so-blessed event. Turmoil became tragedy when he denied that the baby was even his.

"To be rejected and abandoned overwhelmed me with hurt and anger. After two months I aborted my child, and it was, I thought, the happiest day of my life. Finally, I was rid of all traces of the man who had betrayed my love.

"Five years later I rededicated my life to the Lord. It wasn't until then that the shame about the abortion rang loudly in my soul. Not only was I ashamed about the abortion, but I was also ashamed about the happiness I felt afterward. I was a murderer! Guilt, despair, and hopelessness taunted me. God would surely punish me. How could he ever forgive me? How could I ever forgive myself?

"Exhausted with the aching thoughts that continued to torment me and desperately longing to be free, I devoured every book I could find on the topic of healing from abortion. I learned these three life-changing, life-saving facts: First, sin, no matter what the sin, is a selfish act. All sin falls into this category. In God's eyes, sin is sin, and there is no hierarchy. Murder and lying are sins that need the same merciful hand of God. Second, I saw the truth of 1 John 1:9 in a new light. 'If we confess our sins, he is faithful and just and will forgive us our sins and purify us from *all* unrighteousness' (emphasis mine). I had to accept God's forgiveness. And third, I had to grieve the loss of my child.

"I worked through the anger toward my former boyfriend and the anger I felt toward myself. Weeping profusely over the death of my baby was okay, and in so doing, I shed tons of emotional weight. Depression slowly began to dissipate.

"In addition to grieving, I knew that I had to reprogram my mind with the Word of God. Paul calls it 'renewing the mind' (see Rom. 12:2). Reading, reciting, and memorizing Scripture helped the truth take root in my spirit. The mistakes of Moses, David, and Paul reminded me that I was not alone. At last I stopped reminding myself every year of how old my child would have been and what my life would have been like were he alive.

"O the wonder of God's love and forgiveness! As I walk in my healing I know that my baby is in the loving arms of the Father. Before the earth was formed, God anticipated his arrival."

*   *   *

Everyone who stands silently by while this country participates in mass murder by abortion shares in this woman's guilt. As we repent, we too can share in the love and healing that come from God's forgiveness, the result of his amazing grace.

On June 22, 1998, I met Norma McCorvey, the woman in the *Roe v. Wade* Supreme Court decision that made abortion legal in this country. Norma is now a Christian, and she gave her testimony at the Whittier Baptist Church in Whittier, California. She told us that in the 1970s she had been very, very confused. Her life had been "a mess."

Since Norma has given her heart to Jesus Christ, she later confided as we stood together for a photo, that what has impressed her most is the love and acceptance she experiences as she travels to churches across the country. That she is wholeheartedly embraced in the same community that before represented alienation is a constant reminder to her of the all-consuming love of God.

God's love, cleansing, healing, and forgiveness change us. And through his power we accept the responsibility to help change our world. With a better understanding of what is being taught in sex education classes in this nation's schools today, we may have a better idea of where to go from here.

Comprehensive Sex Education

The sex education of the mid-to-late 1970s pales by comparison with the comprehensive sex education taught in our classrooms today. The word *comprehensive* means that *everything about everything* is taught to our children, including masturbation; "outer-sex," which is having sex without going "all the way"; homosexuality; and transsexuality. Most parents are ignorant of what lessons their children are *really* learning at school.

In sex education, suffice it to say students learn all there is to know about the mechanics of self-sex, same-sex sex, and sexual intercourse. The goal is to teach children information that we as parents, churches, and other institutions are not teaching in order to help children develop an "understanding" about their own sexuality. In the process, they are being indoctrinated, or dare we say violated?

Abstinence is not a popular topic in sex education classes. Criticized as teaching that "sex is something to avoid or fear," it is contrasted with comprehensive sex education, which teaches that "sex is a healthy and normal part of life."[12] Abstinence educators and proponents are given labels such as "right-wing," "homophobic," and "fanatics" and are accused of being judgmental, sanctimonious, unrealistic, conservative, dogmatic, biased, preachy, and so on.

Coupled with the classroom doctrine are publications like *Sex, etc.*, a free newsletter written by students who are supervised by so-called health educators and professional journalists. It is circulated to schools across the country, and free copies are given to students three times a year. Parents would be appalled at the content of most of the articles. That schools and youth organizations distribute this material might be an abuse of privilege and responsibility. Many of the topics are distasteful, and to make matters worse, children have access to this organization through the Internet.

* * *

In Chelmsford, Massachusetts, high school students sat prepared for their health lecture. Permission slips were collected. Several students forgot to bring a signed slip from their parents, but the health instructor informed them that it wasn't really necessary. Taking the paper home was a mere formality to ease parental concern.

"Today we are going hear a presentation on sexual health." As the lights dimmed, a woman from a production called Hot, Sexy and Safer began to speak. Much to the amazement of the students and under the guise of promoting "safer sex," the presenter told the students that they were going to have a "grown-up sexual experience" and launched into a lewd monologue about oral sex, homosexuality, and masturbation, even simulating the latter.

The boys were shocked and embarrassed. The girls were repulsed. The health teacher ignored the cries of protest and insisted that this was a normal, natural part of their human development. No one was excused from the classroom. Everyone had to remain inside to watch.

The Condom Race

Sex education classes often include exercises geared to desensitize students. To encourage condom use, for example, teachers aim to reduce embarrassment by providing opportunities for students to handle condoms through in-class demonstrations. One such game is called the Condom Race. Students sit in groups and take turns wearing blindfolds as they roll and unroll condoms on "anatomically correct erect penis models . . . appropriate-sized fruits or vegetables, such as a cucumber, a zucchini, or a banana."[13] The blindfolds are worn because condoms are usually put on in the dark. The team that wins receives colored condoms, buttons, or pins promoting safer sex.

After playing this "game," do students have more confidence handling condoms? Surveys indicate the opposite. Students are still uncomfortable, and who would question why?

Abstinence Works

Research demonstrates that teaching abstinence works. In survey after survey students say that abstinence is what they want to learn. Self-control, self-respect, delayed gratification, planning for the future, and building healthy friendships are essential for every aspect of successful living—not just in the delay of sexual activity. But students are less likely to learn about sexual purity or abstinence in public schools than they are to learn about how to use condoms.

chapter 8

clinics in the schools

If you see the poor oppressed in a district, and justice and rights denied,
do not be surprised at such things; for one official is eyed by a higher one,
and over them both are others higher still.
Ecclesiastes 5:8

Clinics on school grounds are called School-Based Health Centers (SBHCs) or School-Based Clinics (SBCs). The term *clinic* is not preferred by those who promote clinics. They prefer the more palatable term *health center*. Some clinics are not located directly on school grounds, but since they are strategically very close—usually within a block or two—they are called School-Linked Clinics (SLCs) or School-Linked Health Centers (SLHCs).

*　*　*

When the bell rang, fifty-nine sixth-grade girls in East Stroudsburg, Pennsylvania, lined up for class expecting to learn their three R's. With chins held high, they entered their rooms, books securely tucked under their arms, eyes eager with innocent anticipation.

"Today, we are going to make a special visit," the teacher announced. "We're going to see the nurse's office."

Trusting and eager to please, the girls lined up in neat rows and filed into the nurse's office. As each class piled into the room throughout the morning, only a few of the girls became slightly alarmed when they noticed that the door was locked behind them.

"Take off your clothes!" they were commanded. Obediently, they slipped out of their dresses, slacks, skirts, and blouses until they were left standing in just their underwear. The teacher asked for and collected all of their garments.

One by one these preteen, virgin girls were then taken into an inner room where the gynecologist put each onto the examining table, spread her legs with the help of an assistant, and proceeded to perform a genital examination. Not until the first girl screamed out in terror did the others realize that something was terribly wrong.

They began to cry. They begged for their clothes. They pleaded for a chance to call their mothers. Each request was denied.

* * *

When they learned what had happened to their daughters, some parents hired the Rutherford Institute, a law firm, to represent them. The case was settled out of court in favor of these parents, who had contended that the school had violated the girls' constitutional rights.

School-Based Health Centers

In SBHCs, minors can be examined, "evaluated," and prescribed medications. Clinic staff also have the right to transport students off-campus during school hours for abortions[1]—all without parental knowledge or consent. Nurses and doctors in these clinics are immune to otherwise restrictive laws governing local school districts.

School-based health centers are this country's attempt at a comprehensive teenage pregnancy prevention program, which comes under the umbrella of national health care reform.[2] Citing statistics that many children go without physical examinations because they are uninsured, proponents argue for a socialized approach to providing reproductive health care.

Since the majority of these children—African-American and Hispanic—attend public schools, this is the most logical place to serve as "surrogate" parents for the "nation's neediest children."[3] But these "at-risk" students are not the only target for SBHCs. Plans are to have a clinic in *every* public school, including elementary.[4]

The Birth of SBHCs

The birth of school-based clinics began with Margaret Sanger's push to preserve life for the elite class by providing birth control for the masses.[5] Decidedly racist in origins, Planned Parenthood soon became the vehicle to promote this agenda.[6]

By the mid-1960s, controlling births in the black population was a major governmental concern, because African-American women were perceived to be particularly fecund or fertile.[7] To reduce births, the federal government subcontracted Planned Parenthood to set up walk-in, nonmedical units to provide family planning services in neighborhoods populated by minority and poor women.[8] But how would these services be expanded to the schools? Here is the process.[9]

The Commission on Population Growth

In 1970 a special commission was formed—the Commission on Population Growth and the American Future—to study the effects of population growth and immigration on government, the economy, and the environment. This evaluation took place over a two-year period from 1970 to 1972.

Meanwhile, Planned Parenthood considered that sex education was the vehicle to provide contraceptive and birth-control services for teenagers. To spearhead the effort to mandate comprehensive sex education in public school curricula, Mary Calderone resigned as director of Planned Parenthood and established the Sex Information and Education Council of the United States (SIECUS).[10] This self-proclaimed agency is the watch dog for monitoring how sex ed is taught in our nations' schools.

Planned Parenthood's next step was to get its services into public schools.[11] As early as 1970, the first school-based clinic opened quietly in an inner-city school in Dallas.[12] That same year, three hundred females at Yale University were given the "morning-after pill."[13]

Simultaneously, changing existing laws became the focus. With parental notification and consent, providers faced a major roadblock since minors were prevented from receiving contraceptives and birth control unless their parents approved.[14] Something had to change.

The Final Report

In 1972 the Commission on Population Growth and the American Future issued its final report. Stating that the task for fertility-related services was a governmental priority that was too important to be left to voluntary organizations or to private efforts, the commission recommended that our government hire Planned Parenthood Federation of America (PPFA) to manage the nation's family planning.[15]

The agreement was quite costly. Commonly known as Title X, hundreds of millions of dollars ($275 in 1974, $325 in 1975, $400 each subsequent year) were set aside to pay PPFA.[16] As the "expert," PPFA continues to be a hired agency, a subcontractor of the federal government that provides its specialized services—abortion, birth control, and contraception—for the purposes of controlling population growth.

Encourage Women to Work

The Commission's report recommended other significant actions that were to determine the role of Planned Parenthood. It suggested reducing family size by the following:

- *Encourage women to work.* Noting that women who worked outside the home had smaller families, the Commission recommended increasing women's options beyond domestic pursuits. No stereotypical roles were in mind, but rather jobs that would "compete successfully with childbearing beyond the first child."[17]
- *Pass the Equal Rights Amendment.* In order for women to have access to attractive work options, the Equal Rights Amendment had to be passed.
- *Eliminate racial discrimination in employment.* For minorities, recommendations included improving employment, education, and vocational training, and developing low- to middle-income housing.
- *Change parental notification and consent laws.* The Commission urged the Council on State Governments, the American Law Institute, and the American Bar Association to "formulate appropriate statutes" to reverse all laws restricting the availability of all family planning, including laws that pertained to parental notification and consent.[18]
- *Make contraceptives available to minors.* Because schools were accessible to minors, schools were to assume the responsibility of teaching family planning, population control, and sex education, funded by the government.

Condoms and a Second SBHC

By 1972 it was time to take a second look at condoms. They were identified as the best contraceptives for teens, because they were affordable and available without a prescription.[19] Since condoms were for students who were already sexually active, it was decided that condom availability would not encourage sexual activity among teens who were virgins.[20]

In 1973, after a two-year delay due to objections from parents, teachers, and the community, a second school-based health center opened in St. Paul, Minnesota. When the Board of Education finally granted its approval, it was with the stipulation that contraceptives *not* be made available on school grounds. Clinic staff agreed. After the clinic opened, however, contraceptives were distributed.[21]

How SBHCs Work

Planned Parenthood provides the personnel, programs, and birth-control services for all school-based health centers. Private physicians or those who work in teaching hospitals serve as additional staff. To allay concerns from parents, teachers, administrators, and the community about contraceptives being given to students, clinic staff are advised not to dispense contraceptives during the first year of operation but to introduce these services in the second year after the controversy over opening the SBHC subsides.[22]

To avail themselves of additional millions in federal dollars set aside for mental health, antidrug, and antismoking programs, SBHCs also provide these related services. Students are encouraged to enroll in the clinic by staff who offer physicals for athletics, jobs, and college; immunizations; and weight-control programs.[23] Special incentives such as pizza parties and free tickets to school dances and sporting events are additional ways school administrators encourage all students to enroll in the clinic.[24]

Principals and school administrators also assist the SBHCs by giving students' class schedules to the staff so that the nurses can invite students to visit the clinic. Once inside, no matter what the reason for the visit—an ear infection, a cut—all students are asked about their sexual activity and offered birth control and contraceptives. Females receive pelvic examinations and Pap smears, usually during the morning school hours, those times when parents assume their kids are engaged in academics.[25]

Students are also given psychosocial evaluations—mental health tests—again without their parents' notification or consent. The results of these tests are placed in students' school files and may follow them throughout the rest of their years in the educational system. And while regular school nurses cannot give students an aspirin without their parents' consent, nurses and doctors in these health clinics can even prescribe mental health drugs if their psychosocial evaluation so indicates. Why are clinics so powerful, and how did parents lose their rights?

Parental Consent Not Necessary

With the legalization of abortion in 1973, laws regarding access to reproductive services were challenged. The voting age had been lowered from twenty-one to eighteen, which meant that older teenagers could now be recognized as adults and receive comprehensive reproductive health services. However, because younger teens still could not purchase condoms from the local drugstore, parental consent and notification laws were still decidedly in the way.

That changed in 1977. In *Carey v. Population Services International*, the U.S. Supreme Court ruled that contraceptives were to be made available to *all* minors without parental notification or consent, just as the Commission on Population Growth recommended.[26] In other words, with this federal action, parents today are denied the right to give permission or even to be informed about whether their daughter is injected with Norplant—the long-acting contraceptive inserted into the upper arm—has an IUD inserted into her uterus, has a saline or D & E abortion, or is given RU—486, the so-called morning-after pill. It doesn't matter how young she might be.

Neither do parents have to be told if their son has a sexually transmitted disease or if he has been sterilized. *Federal law mandates that parents do not have the right of consent or the right to be informed.*

Utah is the exception. And with the 1980 law requiring parental consent for birth control, teenage pregnancy declined in that state.[27]

Expensive Operations

These school-based health centers are expensive to operate—from $90,000 to more than $300,000 per clinic—and costs are primarily for salaries. A host of private foundations also underwrite costs. Additional monies come from state grants, Medicaid, and social services.[28] It is ironic that in many of these same schools children don't have enough textbooks, writing paper, or computers, yet so much money is dedicated to these clinics.[29]

By 1985 there were 13 SBHCs; by 1986 there were 60 SBHCs with 75 in the planning stages; and by 1988 there were more than 150 SBHCs. With the spread of HIV/AIDS, clinic proponents convinced schools to offer contraceptive services, especially condoms, and local school districts yielded. By 1991 there were 239 clinics on public school grounds.

In 1992 a national plan called for mandatory comprehensive sex education curricula and school-based clinics in *all* schools—elementary, middle, and high, public and private—by the year 2000. Although the goal was not fulfilled by that time, it is still on the agenda.[30] By 1997 there were 948 clinics, and when combined with SLHCs, today the number of clinics that have access to our children reaches well over 1,000 nationwide.

Center for Population Options/Advocates for Youth

There is nothing like a name change to help mask identity. The Center for Population Options was founded to offer technical assistance and advisory support for establishing SBHCs. The agency now has a different name—Advocates for Youth—but its purpose is unchanged.

Surfing through their warm, friendly web site, the sharp observer will uncover a host of propaganda—about promiscuity, lesbianism, homosexuality, and transsexuality—all under the guise of tolerance. Advising on ways to bring SBHCs to local schools, they especially recommend citing poverty statistics and the number of poor children who are without medical coverage. Then they recommend comparing clinic costs to that of private medical care to promote SBHCs as cost-effective vehicles that deliver health services.

Advocates for Youth offers expert advice in how to handle the media, how to respond to parent, teacher, and community confrontation, and how to package services for specific ethnic groups—in short, how to reach the nation's kids.[31]

* * *

Dear Parent/Guardian of [the school and student's name]:

URGENT! PLEASE READ THIS IMMEDIATELY. WE NEED YOUR HELP.

I am trying to make sure your student gets enrolled and receives credit for one or more [school name] courses. I have been informed that [the school] has put a Health Center Hold on your student and I cannot enroll them *[sic]* until that hold is released. The reason for that Health Center Hold are *[sic]*:—[school name] requires students, in the event of an emergency, to have of *[sic]* file in the [school name] Health Center the attached MEDICAL HISTORY AND CONSENT FOR TREATMENT form.

HOW YOU CAN HELP.
Please complete this form and return it in the enclosed envelope to [name of person] at the [school's main office].

I hope this does not provide any inconvenience, and I appreciate your help to assure the safety of your student and that your student will be enrolled in [school name] and receive credit. If I can be of assistance, please contact me immediately at [phone number].

[Signed by Assistant Principal]
The Los Angeles County Office of Education

This form shows the intimidation parents face. Stating that the student won't receive credit for classes, the school urges parents to sign this school-based health center form. Yet parents don't really have to sign. Irving and I never signed the form, yet La Nej was given credit for *every* class.

Instead of signing, it is better to send a letter stating that under no circumstances is your child to be included in any health class where sex education is the topic. Demand that your child be excused. Know your state's laws. Use them as a tool when you review the school's materials. Perhaps abstinence education is an option you can use.

If parental permission is irrelevant, why is it so important to have parents sign the forms? Studies showed that these clinics were failing in their objectives.[32] Pregnancy rates were not declining. Rather, teenage sexual activity was on the rise, not among inner-city poverty teens but among the middle-class white population.[33]

However, huge dollar amounts were at stake. So to prove their effectiveness to the federal government, Planned Parenthood's clinic staff was advised to count the "total number of students with parental consent forms on file." They are also to count the number of students who come into the clinic, no matter the reason for the visit.[34] This numbers game is merely for reporting purposes, and bigger numbers keep the federal dollars and foundation grant monies rolling in.

Paper versus Principles

Meanwhile, abstinence educators and Right-to-Life proponents were losing the battle in this numbers game because they were fighting a paper war with words. Abstinence argued principles. Comprehensive sex education, school-based clinics, and condom availability argued with thick reports, graphs, and figures.

Armed with government grants and thousands of foundation dollars for research, paper after paper and report after report documented the need for more school-based clinics, particularly in underprivileged neighborhoods. Research to counter these findings slowly began to emerge. The timing was right, because by the late 1980s, abstinence was experiencing a revival. A National Adolescent Student Health Survey of 11,000 eighth and tenth graders demonstrated that 94 percent of the females and 76 percent of the males responded that abstinence—how to say no—was what they wanted to learn.[35]

However, another study minimized this finding and suggested that sex educators mix the messages—teach kids to say no while also teaching alternatives for kids who want to be sexually active. Abstinence proponents reasoned that mixing the messages confused teenagers, and research supported this view.[36] Although these were excellent attempts at playing by the rules, research that countered Planned Parenthood's agenda simply was not respected. As school-based health centers continue to expand today—they are already in some elementary schools and plans are to begin comprehensive sex education at the kindergarten level[37]—clinics in our children's schools seem like a giant that's too big to fall.

The 1997 Title V Personal Responsibility and Work Opportunity Act gave a tiny boost to abstinence education when $250 million ($50 million annually) was designated nationally to teach abstinence for five years. The majority of the states complied, but the powerful Planned Parenthood lobby in Sacramento countered in the state of California and said no to this money. Millions of dollars were refused every year, preventing children from learning what other children were benefiting from across the country. The emphasis, instead, was to push for SBHCs in every school.[38]

Today, nationally, abstinence programs are being evaluated, but the research standards are far more stringent than those imposed on research supporting condoms. This means that no matter how successful abstinence education proves to be, on paper it will still be questioned because of researchers who do not want to promote the abstinence message. If abstinence education works, what does that mean for the pro-condom lobby and all those who are receiving monies for clinics and abortions?

Sue the Schools

Lawsuits succeeded in closing some school clinics,[39] but more parents need to become involved in resisting clinic openings, which is admittedly a tough fight. Still, there are too few voices speaking on behalf of the family. Christian organizations are sounding the alarm to a nation that seems very hard of hearing. For whatever reasons, many mothers and fathers are silent.

Parent Power

Parents who are vocal are the ones who realize that they do have power. They begin exercising it with the first visit to their child's school. When there, ask questions, lots of questions! Introduce yourself to the principal and to your child's teachers. Make phone calls and write letters if something disturbs you.

Explain to your child why you do not want him or her to be a part of any sex education in school. Encourage your child to leave the classroom, even if it means being penalized by teachers or administration. Every day when your child comes home from school, ask what happened in each class. If you have developed a relationship of listening and talking with your child, you will have learned to recognize cues that tell you when something is wrong.

Discuss your child's homework assignments. Read the work that has been completed during the school day. Encourage your son or daughter to stand up for his or her faith, and back your child up with your presence at the school whenever necessary.

If public school is your only option, determine to read everything. The beginning of the school year can be hectic, and when a stack of forms is brought home, it is easy just to sign on the dotted line. But don't sign without reading. And don't be intimidated.

What else can be done to protect the family? We'll discuss options in part 3, but first, let's answer the question, "Does sexual intercourse increase in schools with SBHCs?"

chapter 9

condoms—just in case?

Let us behave decently, as in the daytime,
not in orgies and drunkenness, not in sexual immorality
and debauchery, not in dissension and jealousy.
Rather, clothe yourselves with the Lord Jesus Christ, and do not
think about how to gratify the desires of the sinful nature.
Romans 13:13-14

Isn't it a good idea, some may ask, to give kids condoms just in case? After all, with two-thirds of all who contract HIV/AIDS doing so before they're twenty-five, isn't it better to protect children by giving them an alternative to abstinence?

My answer is a resounding no! Clear guidelines are much more effective than the best-intended mixed message.

* * *

Prom was around the corner. After a rocky freshman year that resulted in a change of high schools, La Nej was now focused and doing well in her classes. With plans to attend a Christian college solidly in line, we relaxed and enjoyed the excitement of La Nej's high school graduation.

Well, Irving didn't really relax. He scrutinized every young man who asked La Nej to the prom. He met each one—seven requests in all—and said no to every one.

"But why, Daddy?" The dinner table conversations seemed to go on forever. Irving would explain that there was something he didn't trust about one boy, or that he didn't like the attitude of the other, and on and on it went. Throughout these discussions I was silent. I didn't perceive what my husband did, but I trusted him, and so did his daughter.

The prom was now three weeks away, and La Nej still had no date. "If push comes to a shove, I'll take you myself," he said. And that was that.

What amazed me most throughout this entire process was my child's attitude. I kept expecting her to become belligerent, insistent, or rebellious, but she didn't. With every boy her father rejected, she asked why but never argued the point once he gave his explanation. She showed no anger or animosity, and there was no tension in our home.

Meanwhile, at the university where I taught, graduation was approaching. One of the young women I mentored, Jerilyn, was graduating, and her family was flying from Tennessee to Los Angeles for the ceremony. During the week of graduation everyone came to our home for dinner—Jerilyn, her parents, sister, and brother. What a side-splitting evening we had, trading stories and telling family jokes.

When they left, Irving said to me, "I'd trust Jeremy with my daughter." Jeremy had just completed his freshman year in college and had come home in time to join his family on the trip to Los Angeles. His character testified of his relationship with Jesus Christ and spoke volumes of his upbringing in a fine Christian home. Irving called Jeremy's dad the next day and asked if Jeremy could remain in Los Angeles to escort La Nej to the prom, which now was just days away. The answer was yes.

Irving took Jeremy to rent a tuxedo and a car while La Nej and I shopped for a dress. "You can pick out any dress you like," I told her. "I don't care how expensive it is." We met with little success until her godfather took her shopping at an exclusive store that sold fabulous evening dresses.

It didn't take long for them to find an adorable, above-the-knee, sleeveless red dress. Afterwards, we were caught in a whirlwind of visiting the hair and nail salon, shopping for shoes and makeup, and hunting for the perfect earrings.

After a picture-taking send-off, the house seemed empty and so very, very quiet. I assumed that Irving would wait up for his daughter to come home, and I was prepared to sit up with him.

But Irving went to bed. Confident that La Nej was in good hands, he slept peacefully. And so did I.

The next day La Nej and Jeremy told us how much fun they had at the prom, and they joined some schoolmates that day for a trip to Disneyland. There they learned that prom night wasn't as much fun for everyone—the pressure of the sexual rites of passage left its disappointing tears on many a cheek.

Today La Nej and Jeremy remain friends. Jeremy is now married and recently celebrated the birth of his daughter. Prom night was special for him, too. He didn't go to his own high school prom because of his parents' strong Christian conviction and desire to protect their son from the pressures of his peers. So for Jeremy, La Nej's prom night was a dream come true. Isn't it amazing how God honors his children when they are obedient?

* * *

Ministries that are sensitive of the need for graduates to celebrate the end of high school (while acutely aware of the negative behaviors that attend most proms) might offer an alternative. The Youth Ministry at Crenshaw Christian Center in Los Angeles, for example, hosts an annual teen formal that allows graduates to have fun without the pressures of alcohol, drugs, and sex.

Students in this environment experience positive peer pressure among others whose values and practices match their own. It is good reinforcement, and because of the lack of moral guidelines in our schools, this is an idea more and more parents and their churches are implementing.

Why Religion?

When the Bible was removed from our schools, something else took its place. Humanism is the new religion our children are learning today. Its message is selfish and self-serving. There are no moral absolutes, no standards for what is right and what is wrong. Humanism preaches that anything goes as long as it feels right for the moment. The choices you make don't require anyone else's approval but yours. After all, you are a god. And as such, you don't need God.

A religious system that acknowledges a sovereign God recognizes that he has absolute standards. Through God's Word we are provided with a necessary moral foundation. Children raised in a godly environment realize that as they are obedient to God's Word, it will sustain them, guide them, and give them wisdom to make right decisions. This doesn't mean they will be perfect and not make mistakes, but it does mean that they will be aware of laws that exist outside themselves and for their own good.

Herein lies the difference between the camp that would offer contraceptives to kids and teach kids that they have a choice of alternative lifestyles versus teaching them that there are absolutes about which they are to make the right decisions. This difference is philosophically at the core of our argument, and it is evident in the language we use. The difference is God.

When Children Choose

When children choose, they are selecting from the many options presented to them. It's as if we're telling them that any choice they make is fine and that all choices are equal. But children are not equipped to make such choices. Neither are they equipped to decide whether they will be sexually pure. Why? They do not have all of the facts to make a sound judgment. Therefore, it is *our* responsibility as adults who do have all of the facts not to present our children with a host of options or choices, but to present them with an absolute to which we expect them to adhere. When they are mature enough to make decisions, we then expect them to make the right decision.

In schools today, our children are given choices that wreak havoc on themselves, their families, their communities, and their country. Condom availability is a choice that should not be presented to our kids.

Our children trust us to guard their well-being, to guide their lives, to teach them right from wrong. We say, "This is the correct way to spell." "That is the right way to multiply." "One plus one does *not* equal three. That is wrong."

Once we present children with options, is it unrealistic for them to assume that since we know what is best for them, we are offering them a choice that is equally beneficial? By offering the choice, do we not also imply that it is for their good?

This is why kids today are confused, and we are the ones confusing them. We don't need to offer choices as if anything is acceptable. It's not! We need to present absolutes, right and wrong, and then equip children with the tools they need to make the right decisions.

* * *

I was invited to speak at my daughter's public school. As I was explaining that there is no such thing as "safer sex"—no condom can protect the heart—and that sex is for marriage between a man and a woman only, I was interrupted.

A girl in the front row asked, "Well, what about lesbians? You're talking about marriage, but what about us?"

I looked at this child asking me for an answer. She was confused, and she wanted to know the difference between right and wrong.

"A lesbian lifestyle is wrong," I told her. "God intended sex for married people, a man and a woman."

As she looked back at me, she appeared to be stunned. I wondered if this was the first time an authority figure had given her an absolute answer.

* * *

Counselors are schooled in Project 10, a program that teaches public school counselors to assure students coming to them for help that it's okay to be homosexual.

Pushing the homosexual agenda in schools begins in kindergarten and first grade. One curriculum used in California goes like this: "There are different kinds of families. Some families have a mommy and a daddy. Others have a daddy and a daddy. And still others have a mommy and a mommy."

Although homosexuals comprise less than 1 percent of the population, they are a vocal and effective group. Their tactics include identification with the Civil Rights Movement and claims that their rights are being violated just as rights were denied to blacks prior to legislative intervention. Most African-Americans resent this comparison. Being born black is not akin to choosing whether or not to be gay or lesbian. Any attempt to equate the gay rights movement with the Civil Rights Movement is an affront to the goals and Christian ideals that undergirded the latter's noble purpose.

Like Project 10, condom availability offers students choices. The implication is that any choice is okay. But this choice is wrong for our children. It is wrong for our schools. It is wrong for our communities. It is wrong for America. It is wrong, in fact, for the world.

* * *

Several years ago, my daughter, La Nej, who now lectures to teens on the benefits of sexual purity, worked for an abstinence organization that teaches abstinence in some schools by invitation. She told me this story.

"We were teaching about abstinence in a high school, and they asked us about condoms. We explained why they don't work 100 percent, why they're not guaranteed to be effective against HIV. We showed them the size of the HIV/AIDS virus compared to the size of an actual pore in a condom.

"After our talk, a young man came up to us. He was so confused. He kept asking, 'Why is there so much sex everywhere? Why are we so influenced to have sex if it isn't right? If condoms don't work, if they're not totally effective against HIV, then why are they even handing out condoms here?'

"I understood his frustration but had no real answer for him. What a sad commentary about the teachers and leaders in the educational system."

The AIDS Argument

The HIV/AIDS virus is commonly transmitted by "semen, blood, and vaginal secretions," which enter the body "through the lining of the vagina, vulva, penis, rectum, or mouth."[1] AIDS is the leading cause of death among persons twenty-seven to forty-four. Conservative estimates are that 1 million Americans may be infected, and 36 million people are infected worldwide. Two-thirds of those who contract the virus are under age twenty-five, and one-quarter are adolescents.

When the number of AIDS cases in teenage girls increased 71 percent between September 1989 and September 1990, many schools were making condoms available to students whether or not they had clinics.[2] Schools in Cambridge, Massachusetts, where over 1,500 adolescents were infected with HIV, were the first to adopt condom availability programs, distributing condoms through school nurses or in coin-operated vending machines.[3]

Here's a school district where 1,500 students had already received death sentences. The solution? Give them condoms!

Let's think this through. Planned Parenthood Federation of America has one primary assignment from the federal government: Control the growth of the U.S. population. As a contraceptive, condoms have been proven to be somewhat effective in preventing the sperm from meeting the egg. They are free or relatively inexpensive to purchase, and they do not require a prescription. Therefore, condoms are a simple approach to preventing pregnancies.

Condoms do not, however, *prevent* the spread of the HIV virus; hence the more accurate term "safer sex" as opposed to "safe sex." Condoms are safer than what? Condoms are safer than nothing, but they are not safe, as the writer of the following letter testifies questioning the wisdom of distributing condoms in Washington, D.C., high schools.

July 3, 1992
The Washington Post
1150 15th Street, NW
Washington, D.C. 20071

Editor, . . .
There are facts . . . which suggest that rubber contraceptives are inherently unable to make sex safe. The 12% failure of condoms in the prevention of pregnancy alone argues against their use for preventing contraction of a fatal disease. However, because the AIDS virus is orders of magnitude smaller than sperm, the situation is actually worse. The ASTM Standard D3492 for assessing condom leakage consists of observing an absence of visual leakage . . . when the condom is filled with water. [This test is] inadequate for revealing the presence of holes approaching the dimensions of the AIDS virus [and] provides no assurance that the condom can prevent passage of the virus. Moreover, . . . electron micrographs reveal voids 5 microns in size (50 times larger than the virus), while fracture mechanics analyses . . . suggest inherent flaws as large as the 50 microns (500 times the size of the virus) . . . .

> C. M. Roland
> Editor,
> *Rubber Chemistry and Technology*
> Head, Polymer Properties Section
> Naval Research Laboratory
> Washington, D.C.

Encouraging Promiscuity

Parents who give their students condoms just in case really don't expect their children to remain sexually pure, do they? Approval for sexual intercourse is vicariously implied through the very act of putting condoms in our children's pockets. Worst of all, students are given a false sense of security that they are protected against the potentially lethal virus.

Comprehensive sex education in our classrooms, condoms in our schools, and clinics on school grounds encourage promiscuity. Students are learning socially through observation that sexual intercourse is the norm. Consider this research:

- Young women fifteen to eighteen years old who have had a course in sex education are more likely to have sexual intercourse.[4]
- Pregnancies increase in neighborhoods with family planning clinics.[5]

- Pregnancy rates are significantly higher in clinic schools than in nonclinic schools.[6]

Is there an environment in high schools that encourages sexual activity? Does the presence of the clinic on school grounds and condoms in the classroom convey a message to students that sexual activity is expected and accepted?

These questions were the basis for my doctoral research. To find some answers, an anonymous self-administered Survey of Youth Attitudes from the Institute of Research and Evaluation in Utah was given to 450 African-American inner-city high school students in California during the 1994-95 school year.

These students attended two schools that were only four miles apart. One school had a school-based clinic, and the other school did not. In the nonclinic school, however, students were given condoms in an HIV/AIDS assembly two weeks prior to taking the survey.

The point of this study was not exposure to condoms versus no exposure, but rather degree of exposure. A one-hour school assembly represents minimal exposure to condom availability. By contrast, the school-based clinic is an ongoing, intentional, educational intervention differing in magnitude, intensity, size, duration, expense, and degree of exposure to sex education, condom availability, and instruction. This degree of exposure to the safer sex message represents maximum exposure.[7]

Procedures

Parents and guardians signed permission slips that students returned to their homeroom teachers. Color-coded surveys—yellow for the clinic school, blue for the nonclinic school—were given to teachers to administer in their classrooms during a period designated by the teacher.

Students were instructed to discontinue the survey at any time if they felt uncomfortable. Since the survey was made available to the entire student populations, students in each school had equal opportunity to complete the survey. It can be assumed that the 450 students who turned in completed questionnaires—141 students in the clinic school and 309 students in the nonclinic school—were comparable.

Findings

Here is a summary of findings.

1. *Female sexual activity rates are higher in the clinic school.* More females in the clinic school became sexually active, transitioning from virgin to

nonvirgin status, than did females in the nonclinic school, 60 percent versus 37 percent respectively. There was no significant difference among the males.

2. *Males perceive that schools accept and expect sexual intercourse.* Males in both schools agreed that, "If schools give out condoms, it must be okay to have sex," and "If my school gives out condoms, it's because they expect students to have sexual intercourse." Females in both schools disagreed.

3. *The school-based clinic creates a sexually permissive school environment.* There was a significant difference in perceptions between males in the clinic school and males in the nonclinic school. Males in the clinic school *especially* perceived that they were expected to have sexual intercourse more so than did males in the nonclinic school.

4. *Pressure to have sexual intercourse is greater in the clinic school.* Sexually active males and females in the clinic school reported that there was greater peer pressure to have sexual intercourse than did sexually active students in the nonclinic school.

5. *There is no difference in pregnancy rates or STD testing.* Between schools, pregnancy rates and rates for testing sexually transmitted diseases were similar.

6. *In the clinic school, students are less likely to discuss sex with their parents.* Students in the clinic school are less inclined to talk with their parents about sex or to share their parents' values regarding sex than are students in the comparison school.

7. *Students who attend church are more likely to disagree with the "safer sex" message.* Students who attended church one or more times a week disagreed that "Teenagers are safe from contracting the HIV/AIDS virus if they use condoms." Teenagers who attend church are more likely to affirm, "I would not have sexual intercourse even if I had a condom."

Discussion

Although the school-based clinic's goal is to reduce sexual activity, its presence on school grounds may establish sexual activity as the norm. The clinic may send social cues—messages implied in the environment—that it is acceptable for students to have sexual intercourse. This may explain why more female virgins became sexually active in the clinic school than in the nonclinic school. Other studies concur. Access to family planning services "may suggest to teens a greater community tolerance for sexual activity."[8]

Since condoms are a male contraceptive, it is understandable that males in both schools especially respond to this intervention. Handing out condoms in classrooms may imply that the principal, administrators, and teachers approve or accept sexual intercourse among teens. This message is reinforced again and again with the availability of more and more condoms.

While males in both schools perceived that they had permission to have sex, males in the clinic school especially perceived their school environment to be sexually permissive. Apparently, condom availability coupled with the presence of a clinic sends social cues to males even though, traditionally, family-planning clinics service more females than males.

It's no wonder. For adolescents, school is an extension of the peer group. "It provides the standards and status," is a "social map," and "sets the moral standards and situational ethics" for students.[9]

Because these clinics are located on school grounds and appear to function as part of the school, students may perceive the clinic as an extension of their learning environment. It doesn't require huge leaps of logic to understand that condoms in classrooms and clinics on school grounds may communicate to kids that they have "permission for early sexual activity."[10]

Additionally, when parents don't communicate to their children, they are sending messages as well. Studies show that parents' attitudes do affect males' decisions about whether or not to become sexually active.[11] For females, early sexual activity is related to a breakdown in parental communication.[12] In this study, students in the clinic school—especially the males who perceived their school to be a sexually permissive environment—were less inclined to communicate with their parents. Perhaps they realized that since they didn't need parental consent for condoms and since the girls could visit the clinic without telling their parents, there wasn't much left to discuss.

Are Clinics Effective?

Is there a difference in contraceptive use among students who have clinics right on their school grounds? Does contraceptive use increase when sexually active students have easy access through the clinic? A study by researchers who encourage schools to have clinics found that the answers to both of these questions was an overwhelming no.

"The availability of contraceptives on site, which has been thought to be an important convenience factor contributing to positive contraceptive adoption, was not found to be significant."[13] There is no significant relationship between on-site provision of contraceptives through school-based clinics and consistent contraceptive use among high school students. In other words, clinics on school grounds do not encourage sexually active students to use contraceptives.

Furthermore, "Contraceptive use is not related to whether contraceptives are dispensed on site, whether health education and counseling are provided by a health educator, whether contraceptive services are part of a comprehensive array of services that include medical or counseling services, or whether a family planning visit results in the dispensing of contraceptives or a prescription for contraceptives."[14] With all of the money that's put on the table to support these clinics, providing contraceptives, counseling, and other services made no difference whatsoever in students' use of contraceptives.

So why are these clinics still in our schools? And why are there still plans to put school-based clinics or school-based health centers into *every* school?

Teach Abstinence

It is difficult to understand why promoting abstinence was not the chosen HIV/AIDS intervention in major school districts even though researchers determined that abstinence education is effective.[15] And abstinence education is even more effective when those who teach it actually believe it.[16] Students observe models—parents, teachers, peers—and the opinions of those people can be influential in altering students' behavior. The more status a model has, such as that of a teacher, the more influence he or she has.[17]

Rather than teaching kids resistance skills—such as how to say no—as some experts suggest,[18] condoms are being recommended for *every* grade level. It is also recommended that students role-play putting on condoms.[19] Surveys, however, show that these recommendations go against what parents want. Parents favor abstinence education.[20] But the Sex Information and Education Council of the United States considers that curricula emphasizing monogamous heterosexual marriage is inadequate.[21] That is why implementing abstinence education nationwide required a special effort.

The arguments against teaching abstinence begin with the distorted assumption that since all teenagers are going to be sexually active anyway, why not teach them how? Abstinence education is viewed as teaching only one message, while comprehensive sex education is viewed as multifaceted.

Abstinence education is categorized as failing, fear-based, and medically inaccurate, while comprehensive sex education is considered successful. Already it is implied that the Title V abstinence programs deprive kids access to important information, such as how to use condoms. Why else are questions about condoms on the questionnaires that are being used to evaluate abstinence education? Key to maintaining a foothold in our schools is labeling the "abstinence until marriage message" as a religious idea that violates separation of church and state.[22]

With the Title V program evaluation, research outcomes may indicate that teaching kids resistance skills doesn't work. But to the contrary, it *does.*

Best Friends

Based on mentoring teenage girls, Best Friends has been honored as one of the nation's most effective abstinence programs by the National Campaign to Prevent Teen Pregnancy. As many as 4,500 girls in middle school and high schools participate in the program during the school year. The program has a high school graduation rate of 100 percent, and less than 1 percent of females have become pregnant.[23]

Clearinghouse on Abstinence Education

Best Friends is just one example of a successful program. For more information about other programs and curricula, contact the National Abstinence Clearinghouse at *www.abstinence.net*. They will help you select curriculum that's right for your school and your students.

Happily, several excellent resources for abstinence education are available. Teachers might consider A. C. Green's six-week curriculum, *I've Got the Power Abstinence Curriculum for Middle and High School Students.*[24] This interactive material can be taught separately or integrated with subjects such as English, math, composition, history, computer science, and the arts. *The Game Plan* by Project Reality also features A. C. Green and is another great resource.[25] And probably one of the best curricula in the abstinence field is *Teen-Aid.*[26] It is impossible to list all of the abstinence resources here, but two that also deserve to be mentioned are Focus on the Family's *No Apologies* and *The Road Ahead* by Awareness, Inc.[27]

Character education curricula also help students make wise decisions about abstinence. Notable is *AEGIS* by Stan Weed. Also, according to the Christian Educators' Association International, these are among the best: Gene Bedley's curriculum for elementary students has been used in over four thousand schools; *The North American Education Center* by Vernie Schor is for kids in grades K-8; *The Jefferson Institute Materials* is for middle school; the *I Can* series is for elementary through high school; and *Power Connections* by the Medical Institute for Sexual Health is for inner-city middle school students. These can be obtained from the Christian Educators Association International[28] or from the Character Education Partnership.[29]

What Parents Can Do

Parents must lobby their schools and insist on abstinence education. Become an active member of the Parent-Teacher Association, but don't be surprised at the pressure this group asserts to support school-based health centers and condom availability. Be prepared to be in the minority, but be a voice.

Parents can also volunteer to teach or "guest lecture" on abstinence, and some teachers might welcome recommendations on curricula. Pray for your students' schools, and especially pray for Christian teachers in public schools who are the *real* missionaries in America. Ask your church to support a school and pray for teachers.

If it is impossible to change the public school system, parents must place their children elsewhere. Condoms and clinics are not yet in private schools. If all else fails, here are some suggestions:

1. *Home school your children.* When in doubt, take them out! Teach your children at home. Curricula and assistance are available on the Internet with dozens of listings under *www.homeschool.com*.

2. *Start a school in your church.* We need more schools that are free to integrate the Bible into the curriculum. The Association of Christian Schools International (ACSI; see *www.acsi.org*) can help. Accreditation, administration, certification, early education, financial services, legal services, urban services, and advice on salaries and tuition are just some of the topics ACSI offers advice on for churches. With thousands of churches empty during the day—and heat and electricity paid for—the most difficult task is already accomplished. You will be amazed at how easy it is to start a school.

3. *Vote yes for school vouchers.* School vouchers offer parents school choice by allowing them to designate that funds be given to the school they feel best educates their children. Private Christian or church-run schools are options that parents can choose under the school voucher program. Here's how it works: Parents turn in vouchers to the school at the start of the school year, and the school in turn sends in the vouchers to the state to receive funds for every child enrolled. Vouchers are not checks. In other words, parents cannot "cash" a voucher and keep the money for themselves. The argument that a school voucher program will result in the abandonment of public education and leave behind those students who need public schools the most is ludicrous. With vouchers in place, public schools must improve to compete for students. All families benefit from choosing the best school for their kids. Poor families benefit most, because vouchers give them power. No longer are they stuck with sending their children to the school down the street. They can now choose private education, and private education means that parents have more control over what is being taught to their children. Don't be

distracted by the argument that vouchers give rich people money for private schooling. The rich are *already* sending their children to private schools.

4. *Consider independent schools.* An independent school model is Edison schools. Their objective is to improve education by privatization for profit. As incentives, teachers are given stocks, and they become shareholders. As schools become successful, everyone involved profits from the school's success.

Any combination of these solutions is better than subjecting children to the current reproductive health care school system. Will it take the dismantling of public education to effectively topple the network that has unlimited access to our nation's children? Public schools can become the institutions they are supposed to be—learning institutions, not sites for clinics—when competition encourages improvement.

Find out if there are health clinics in your children's schools. Find out what is being taught in health education. Find out if condoms are being given to students or are "made available" by being placed in baskets in the bathrooms. If any of the above exists, find an alternative, and take your children out of public school. You have my permission!

chapter 10

children at risk

Do not be misled: "Bad company corrupts good character."
1 Corinthians 15:33

Drinking, drugs, and delinquency—these behaviors describe children at risk. Sometimes, just as troubling to parents as deviant actions are bad attitudes.

* * *

The neighborhood high school wasn't our first choice, but Irving and I thought it might be okay. Signs that we were wrong were evident when La Nej came home day after day with a negative attitude. Rather than spending time with us, she preferred to stay in her room, which was a marked change in her normal behavior.

The first problem at school was an English teacher who happened to be extremely unpopular with the students. Mrs. X returned my daughter's typed paper all marked up and void of one encouraging comment. I went to school the next day to see her, paper in hand.

"The children in *that* class have small brains," she said without hesitation. "The children in my *other* English class are smart."

I didn't bother continuing any conversation with her but went immediately to the principal's office. "Pull my daughter's test scores," I demanded. "Why is she in that English class with Mrs. X?"

Needless to say, before long, La Nej switched into another class and she faced the rest of the semester with a new teacher. I ached for the children stuck in her former class—mainly Latino and African-American kids—and wondered why the school tolerated Mrs. X at all.

When Black History Month rolled around, we faced problem number two. Since there were only ten or eleven African-American children in the school, Black History Month was a low priority. The teacher assigned to assist these students agreed with them that they should have a dance with the theme "One Nation in the Groove!"

"That's an insult to every African-American who sacrificed his or her life for freedom and equality," my husband and I protested. The next day I went to school again. This time I sat in with the students and their advisor and helped them design an assembly that would educate the entire school body.

A local gospel choir from Biola University came to sing. An actress relayed Sojourner Truth's famous speech, "Ain't I A Woman?" And at intervals students themselves did readings from poems along with portions of speeches from Dr. Martin Luther King Jr. and others.

The assembly was a success, but problems quickly surfaced. All five of the African-American girls—my daughter included—started a clique. They dressed alike and went everywhere together. La Nej's attitude soured.

I invited the other four girls over for dinner to learn a little more about them. We soon learned why they were so angry. None of the girls was living with her birth mother. This was the common bond. And while La Nej's situation was decidedly different from theirs, it was easy for her to empathize.

I realized the problems were too complicated for a quick fix. Rather than trying to change the peer environment, Irving and I made a decision to remove our child from that school. The principal pleaded with us to change our minds because he was so grateful that parents were actually involved with the students. But we felt responsible to God for the child he had given us and opted for the transfer.

We placed La Nej in an arts high school. Here the peer pressure was different. Studying hard, making good grades, and excelling in the arts were the norm. Her attitude adjusted immediately. This was the right decision for our family.

* * *

When kids fall into the wrong peer group, the struggle at home is like swimming upstream. Whatever the common denominator happens to be, it's difficult to convince teens to change their friends, even when they realize that this group isn't good for them. What's a parent to do?

Changing the child's environment is not always possible, but if it is, doing so is a good solution. Moving to a new area, finding a new school, and avoiding certain crowds may seem like extreme measures, but they work. During teenage years, peer group is important, so why not decide which peer group will have the most influence on your child? Bad attitudes are just the beginning of a downward spiral of behaviors that place children at risk for bad habits that ultimately can be devastating.

Kids at Risk

This nation has decided that all of our children are "at risk." Everyone, not just kids in the inner city, is at risk of drug abuse, smoking, drinking, and nonmarital sexual activity.

While the label seems innocent at first glance, at-risk children need special services—like those provided by school-based health clinics—to address their special needs. The rationale for SBHCs in all schools, including elementary, is couched in this innocuous language that targets all kids everywhere.

If we are a nation whose children are at risk, what does this say about the parents? Perhaps students need to complete report cards and bring these to school telling the "authorities" about their parents' behaviors. Parents who are delinquent in their duties can then be monitored and reprimanded.

It's already happening! It may sound far-fetched, but in some schools, students are actually given report cards to evaluate their parents' ability to parent. Students complete and return these to their teachers or to the clinic staff in their schools. Does your child have the secret assignment of completing a report card on you?

Importance of Parental Influence

Researchers have long been aware of the importance of parental influence on their children's behavior. One study evaluated the importance of parental influence on adolescent risk behaviors of alcohol and tobacco use.[1] Was peer group more influential than parents?

"There is reason to believe that the prevention field may have unwittingly overstated peer and understated parental influence,"[2] say the researchers. In effect, it's parents' behavior, what they model to their children, and whether or not parents discuss their feelings about these behaviors that have the most influence.

Parents also exert influence on adolescent smoking and drinking decisions through the messages they send about these behaviors, both explicitly, through their discussions and admonitions regarding substance abuse, and implicitly, through their silence about these issues and their children's behavior. When parents talk with their children about the dangers of alcohol and tobacco, they are not only offering information, they are also providing a clear statement of their opposition to their children's use of substances and of the significance the parents attach to this behavior.

Conversely, when parents fail to talk with their children, the child may view the absence of discussion as an indication that experimentation with alcohol and tobacco is not that important to their parents. Indeed, adolescents who expect that their parents will be unhappy if they use alcohol and tobacco appear less likely to do so.[3]

The authors cite research suggesting that a "no-nonsense" style of parenting among African-American families is responsible for low rates of youthful substance abuse. "Parents are more likely to abstain from using alcohol themselves, as well as more likely to instruct children to abstain."[4]

Parents' influence does not diminish as their children get older. The authors conclude that with family influence so vital in adolescent decision making, school-based prevention programs may have been oversold. That is good news.

This important editor's note follows the research paper:

> The review demonstrates the importance of parental roles in adolescent substance abuse. The public health campaigns promoting communication about drugs, tobacco, and alcohol are on the right path. Some parents struggle with how to tell their child or teen not to do what they have done. As professionals who serve adolescents, we need to encourage parents to be honest about their history while setting firm expectations for avoidance and clear sanctions for unacceptable substance use behaviors.[5]

Children select peer groups that are more likely to engage in the same behaviors they choose for themselves. In other words, birds of a feather *choose* to flock together. And wrong peer groups equals wrong behaviors.

Kids who experiment with drinking and drugs are more likely to engage in other risky behaviors, such as nonmarital sexual activity. With dulled senses, guards are down and judgment is flawed. Parents who understand the value of helping their children stay sober should feel more empowered to do so. And if staying sober is modeled, it is more likely to be followed.

This same advice is feasible to help kids avoid nonmarital sexual activity. The two issues—parents' modeling in the home and talking about their values—are equally effective here.

Testing the Limits

A study of 90,000 kids who are most likely to drink, smoke, have sex, or commit suicide concludes that these children have two things in common—bad grades and too much time hanging out.[6] With free time and lack of supervision, probably the result of parents who are working or otherwise engaged, kids are left on their own. In my study, girls in middle school whose parents worked became sexually active probably because there was no one at home to monitor their behavior.

Belligerent daughters who flex their independence intimidate some mothers, and some single moms simply cannot handle teenage sons with deep voices who tower over them. These children realize that they can make their own rules and openly defy the ones set for them.

Kids who test the limits decide that they—and not their parents—are in control. These children are not necessarily committing criminal acts, but their behavior is rebellious, and they are out of control. Skipping school, speaking disrespectfully to parents, and breaking curfews are examples of unacceptable behavior. Some parents, afraid of losing their children's love and feeling powerless, crumble under the pressure and hand over the reins to their ill-prepared children.

* * *

After teaching a seminar at a local church this fall, I was stopped in the aisle by a European woman who was visibly distraught. "Please, I don't know what to do about my daughter," she said. "Adrienne is fifteen years old, and until a few weeks ago she was an agreeable child. We had a very good relationship. Adrienne used to prefer staying at home practicing her harp, but everything changed when she made a new friend at school named Pauline."

This mother explained how drastically Adrienne's habits had changed. She preferred hanging out at Pauline's house rather than coming home from school. With every new limit her parents set, she disobeyed and pushed harder, threatening to run away if she didn't get her way. Her parents didn't like the lifestyle of Pauline's family, and they worried that Adrienne might be picking up bad habits.

"I feel helpless," the mother continued. "I don't know what to do. She is so angry with me. She won't listen, and I don't want her to hate me. I don't want to lose her."

The night that Adrienne's father refused to let her go out, Adrienne shouted her intentions to leave the house permanently. The tactic worked, and her parents backed off, afraid of losing their daughter forever. After that, Adrienne set the rules. She decided where she would go and when she would return home. Dutifully, her mother would drive to pick her up whenever she called.

I looked at this little woman and sensed her distress. Her daughter had not only lost all interest in music but seemingly all interest in God as well. She refused to attend the morning seminar at the church, preferring instead to hang out with some friends. She told her mom that she would call when she was ready to come home.

"I know how painful it is to be at odds with your child," I said to her. "It feels as if your heart is breaking, and it's a very, very difficult place to be. But you are the mother, and she is the child. God intended that there would be a generation gap for a purpose, and that's because adults are aware of dangers that children can't perceive."

I explained that it was a mother's responsibility to protect her child, and she could only do that by establishing boundaries. "Make rules, and stick to them. Adrienne is the child. She is living under your roof, and you are paying for her food, clothing, and medical care. She is to be subject to you."

After a forty-five-minute encouragement session, I offered some specific instructions. "Go and get your child now. Tell her that you are the parent, and these are the rules. Don't worry about being her friend. And don't worry if she doesn't like you. She may not like you, but she must respect you. Rather than reacting to what your daughter does, I suggest that you take back the reins. Stop feeling powerless."

I also suggested that she speak with more authority. "Why is your voice so soft? Why do you sound so weak?" I asked. I taught her the teacher technique of speaking from the diaphragm so that she could project her voice. She practiced, and we prayed.

Today I telephoned for an update.

"Your prayer and godly advice strengthened me, and God gave me wisdom through you," said a strong voice on the other end of the phone. "I did what you suggested. After I left the church I went to get my daughter. I told her that I was the parent and she was the child, and that she had to obey me.

"It was terrible! She told me that she hated me and that I was the worst mother in the whole world. She screamed that she was never going to forgive me and never going to talk to me. It was a most difficult time, but I didn't back down. Things got worse before they got better.

"After about two weeks, she started to talk to me little by little, and she started telling me things. It has been a couple of months, and now she says that I'm the best mom in the whole world. She wants to hug me and walk arm in arm when we go to the mall! I'm so happy God sent you into my life. I felt as if God was scolding me. He really talked to me through you, and it gave me so much strength and boldness."

What surprised us both was Adrienne's comment about her friend Pauline.

"Adrienne said that Pauline's mom doesn't care about Pauline because she lets her do anything she wants to do. I was shocked the day she hugged me and said that she knows I care about her." What an interesting observation about a child who was given unlimited freedom. It did this mother good to hear her daughter articulate these feelings so clearly.

Adrienne's mother continued, "I don't know what happened exactly. I told her that later on she would thank me for what I did, and perhaps she thought about it or talked with someone else—I don't know. But our relationship was never as good as it is now. I am strong—if I say no, that means no! I think God allowed this to happen purposely because he changed me and made me a different person, and he changed her.

"Adrienne respects me more! I'm stronger, and she knows I'm the mother. I'm the boss, not her! I'm the one running the house." I could hear her confident smile.

I asked about Pauline. "She's still friends with her, but they're not that close. Adrienne is back to playing the harp and practicing a lot more. She has decided that this is what she wants to do for her career."

Before I hung up the phone, I offered another suggestion. "Why not take Adrienne to a Christian university with an excellent music department? Let her spend a weekend on the campus during their student orientation and give her a taste of college life. This way you can help her with a goal for the future, and this incentive may help her stay on track. Who knows? If she keeps practicing, she may even win a full scholarship to the university." Our conversation ended with a prayer of thanksgiving.

* * *

Often, the key to turning behavior around is catching it early. It is more difficult to reverse a pattern that has become a habit. There is no simple way, no easy answer, when kids want to take control. Praying for wisdom and being one step ahead of your child are two suggestions.

* * *

I don't remember the details of the disagreement, but La Nej was throwing a tantrum about my decision. She screamed that she was leaving and stormed into her room and started packing.

I wasn't quite sure what to do. La Nej obviously felt backed into a corner, and this was her way of saying so. I couldn't back down; nor could I let her leave. I prayed and thought. She was almost finished packing.

"Take everything that I bought you out of your suitcase. If you're going to pack, pack the clothes that you paid for." At age fifteen, La Nej hadn't bought very much with her own money.

"Well then I might as well not go," she fumed. "I won't have any clothes."

When Irving came home that evening, I told him what happened. He didn't appreciate the fact that La Nej wanted to retaliate by packing and leaving. I could hear the conversation down the hall.

"I understand that you were packing and intended to leave this house. We're responsible for you until you're eighteen, so if you don't want to be here, we'll decide where you will live. Now you can start packing, because you're going to that boarding school."

I won't mention the name of the school, but I will tell you this. A friend of ours sent his daughter to this school in the South when she started acting out at home. She stayed there six months. Rules were that every student had to rise at 5:00 A.M. and go to work on the school's farm. After classes there were chores to do until evening—no play time. The students studied and worked. This child returned home, stayed on the straight and narrow path, finished high school, and recently graduated from college. She is a model child.

La Nej knew what her friend had gone through, and now she was headed to that same school. When Irving came back into our bedroom, he told me to get the phone number and call the school.

"Please don't send me there!" A repentant child stood in the threshold, her tear-stained face pleading for mercy. "I'm sorry about the way I've been acting." The apology opened the door to a lengthy discussion between La Nej and her dad. Irving reviewed the entire day's events and asked her to think about her actions. He asked La Nej what she could have done instead of packing. After a lengthy talk, we ended in prayer with the three of us holding hands.

* * *

Unfortunately, it may not take long before some kids cross the line from testing the limits to doing a criminal act. Perhaps when mothers and fathers allow their kids to suffer the consequences of their behavior, they will find support and helpful resources in the process. A single mom who personally experienced the trauma of dealing with her son who went beyond the boundary lines found help in the system.

* * *

"My son had gone a step beyond *wanting* to be in control. He had actually *taken* control, and I had no legal recourse to make him stay home. Law enforcement couldn't make him obey me either, because he had not committed a crime.

"At thirteen my son is as tall as I am. If he said he was going out the door and I said no, I couldn't stop him. I had no recourse. Incorrigible kids are in the most dangerous place because they're not accountable to anyone. Unless they break the law and the local law enforcement intervenes, they're pretty much on their own.

"Incorrigible kids do not respond to counseling alone; talking doesn't work, because they don't listen and won't obey. They break all the rules. Suggestions are almost a mockery, because these kids won't do anything you tell them to do, and the law can't make them.

"If you can stop this behavior before they realize the full weight of their independence, you have a chance. Otherwise, if they get a taste of the freedom they have, it's only the grace of God, prayer, and wisdom that will bring them back. Even as a Christian woman, I was frightened and humiliated. These children only respond to consequences, and I was limited to the kinds of consequences I could enforce. For example, if I said 'You're grounded,' and he left anyway, what could I do?

"Aside from praying up a storm, I went on an incredible search to find out what kind of help there was for my child. I was trying desperately to save his life. I checked every agency to find out what programs were in place, but even when I found the right program, I couldn't make him go.

"The most empowering thing I did was to talk to a probation officer who arrested my fear by educating me. It was inevitable that my son was going to do something criminal because of the friends he chose, and the officer recommended actions I could take in the event that this happened. As God would have it, the same day of this three hour session, my son left home.

"I called the police and insisted that my son be listed as a runaway. That did it! He was arrested for tagging (writing on the walls of a building), but because of his age, they called me to pick him up. I refused, saying, 'He did something wrong; let him suffer the consequences.'

"So the police took him to juvenile hall, and he called me every day to come and get him. That's when I had to disassociate from being a rescuing mother. I let him stay for a week, and that made a profound impression on him. He had a court hearing, and the judge made certain stipulations for his return home. Additional consequences can be enforced, because the judge, the district attorney, and the probation department backed me up.

"Before, it was just me against him. I was wrong, and his peers were right. I'm not suggesting that anyone have a child arrested; but allow him or her to suffer the consequences that are appropriate for the behavior.

"Now my son is home, and he respects the boundaries because he has to. This means that if he refuses to be obedient, he can get counseling or he can go to camp. Just having these consequences is enough to make him act responsibly. I'm empowered. Weekend boot camp, counseling, curfews, not associating with certain kids—I got all of this when he entered the system."

* * *

The teen violence hotline is one resource for parents. Call information for a number in your area. They offer advice and are committed to staying on the line until they are able to help. Parents can find additional help through the local probation department.

Some kids are at risk, but certainly not *every* child in *every* public school in the United States! Subjecting elementary, middle, and high school children to mental health evaluations, possibly prescribing drugs, and registering them in school-based health centers is intrusive on the rights of the family. Would you agree?

part 3

churches:
the mandate is to
teach

*Train the younger women to love their husbands
and children, to be self-controlled and pure.*
Titus 2:4–5

The kids were having a sex seminar at the church.
Usually, as pastor of Christian education, it was my
task to plan the evening, contact the speakers, and
arrange for the music. This year was different. When
asked to plan the seminar, I suggested that the students plan it themselves.

I stood in the back and watched the room fill
with teenagers. The music was great, and the speakers were superb. With joy I watched the young leaders buzzing around and taking charge, answering
questions, challenging the students, and encouraging them to be sexually pure. It was evident that the
younger teens looked up to the older ones with a certain reverence and, I think, eternal appreciation.

One leader in particular especially warmed my
heart. She had attended all of my sex seminars and
listened to all of my lectures. Now she was the leader
for tonight's event. I watched her in amazement. She
seemed so grown up. Wasn't it only yesterday that I
flew to New York to get her?

La Nej carries on the legacy of teaching kids to
be sexually pure. She even has her own forum speaking to junior high and high school kids in churches
and schools about the importance of remaining sexually pure. Irving and I couldn't be prouder!

chapter 11

God's standard is abstinence

It is better not to vow than to make a vow and not fulfill it.
Ecclesiastes 5:5

Religion *is* important. Children who attend church one or more times a week are less likely to engage in nonmarital sexual inter-course.[1] If research demonstrates that attending church one or more times a week makes a difference, why not recommend that *more* children go to church or synagogue? Just a thought....

While others are running around in circles trying to dismiss the significance of these results, pastors and youth workers should take heed. A great opportunity is missed by not being more intentional in teaching our children and youth—and adults for that matter—to be sexually pure. Tragedy occurs when young people sit in the pews but no one bothers to teach them about sex from God's point of view.

* * *

Lynn Chamberlain was enjoying her junior year of college. During semester break, she would fly home to see her mother, Marilyn, visit her new boyfriend, then dash back to campus ready to buckle down for more study.

Lynn was in love, and talk of marriage was in the air. She had the key to her boyfriend's place and felt that they were one step from the altar. He was so attentive, and life seemed perfect.

But during her senior year, Lynn began to feel more tired than usual. She alarmed her roommates when, on some mornings, she couldn't even get out of bed. The flu-like symptoms persisted, so she decided that on her next trip home she would see her doctor.

The office visit was rather routine. Everything seemed normal, but just to make sure, Lynn asked for an HIV/AIDS test. A week later her doctor called and asked that she and her mother come into his office. They did.

When the doctor entered the examination room to talk with Lynn and Marilyn, the nurse popped her head in and summoned him for an emergency in another room. He left, promising to return as quickly as possible.

Impatient, Lynn glanced at the folder the doctor had left in the room. She hesitated just a second, and then opened it. She saw the words "HIV TEST POSITIVE."

The word, "Positive" hit her like a death sentence. She screamed and screamed and screamed and screamed. Marilyn ran to her, and when her eyes read what her daughter's eyes had read, she screamed too. Lynn passed out.

The rest of the visit was a blur. The doctor's reassuring words of comfort did little to remove the daggers from Lynn's heart. She sat stunned and in shock. Marilyn wailed over the fate of her one and only child. For her too it felt that life had ended.

"But how? Where did I get this from?" The question kept replaying in her mind until she determined to find an answer. Without announcing her intentions, Lynn went to her boyfriend's apartment while he was at work and let herself in with the key he had given her. She wasn't sure what she was looking for, but she was looking for something.

Lynn started searching everywhere. Bathroom cabinets, under the sink, the nighttable drawer—her search yielded nothing. Refusing to give up, she looked at the chest of drawers securely stacked against the wall. A knot came into her throat. She walked slowly toward what seemed like a mountain, fearing the truth hidden inside.

Lynn opened the first drawer. Nothing. She opened the next, then the next. When she came to the drawer with her boyfriend's underwear, she gently lifted his clothes. Beneath the sparkling white and neatly folded garments were stashed numerous bottles of pills.

Holding the medicines, Lynn sank to the floor and sobbed. "He said that he loved me. How could he do this to me?"

Weak from despair and desperate to find an answer, she waited for her boyfriend to come home. He was his usual cheerful self until she told him of her diagnosis and confronted him with his medicines.

Yes, he was HIV positive, and, yes, he had known for some time. He lived a bisexual lifestyle, which he had kept carefully and conveniently hidden from her. When pressed to tell all, he admitted that he was, in fact, fully aware that he had full-blown AIDS when he first met Lynn.

What could she say to such deliberate deception? Lynn thought that she couldn't hurt any more, but the pain went deeper still. Somehow she managed to drive home.

Marilyn was furious when she learned of her daughter's discovery. Lynn, feeling the full weight of her circumstances, went straight to bed. Without saying a word to her daughter, Marilyn unpacked her gun, loaded it, and drove to Lynn's boyfriend's apartment.

He wasn't home. Marilyn returned to her car and sat and waited. And she waited and waited. Well past midnight he still had not come home. She waited until morning, but still there was no sign of him. Emotionally and physically drained, Marilyn decided to go home. Later she thanked God that her vengeful excursion had failed.

Days, weeks, and months later, Lynn was still in bed. For her, life was over. She wrapped herself in a blanket of depression and waited for the end.

Marilyn, however, threw herself into a whirl of activity. She cleaned and rearranged and cleaned some more. She tried to inspire her daughter to go shopping, to just get out of the house for a bit, but nothing worked.

Not one to give up easily, Marilyn researched HIV/AIDS organizations. Light entered her world when she met Ann Copeland, head of Women at Risk, an AIDS service organization for women. Ann came by the house, spent time with Lynn, and for the first time in months, Lynn got out of bed. Lynn credits Ann for giving her hope and for helping her to look forward to living rather than dying.

Lynn the victim became Lynn the victor. Deciding to go public with her story, she told her pastor, who embraced her and became one of her closest confidants. The congregation, however, was not so accepting. It was the late 1980s, and church people were as ignorant of HIV/AIDS as the rest of the world. Lynn could stretch out on a pew all by herself, because people were afraid to sit next to her. They were also afraid to hug her or to shake her hand.

Talking about her diagnosis and educating the church community were Lynn's strongest medicines. As she became known around the country, Lynn was invited by major football leagues to talk to their players, and she decided that when she traveled with this assignment, she would have a little fun.

Once she arrived in a city where she was to speak, Lynn found the local hangout for the team she was to address. With her tall, lithe frame, beautiful face, and close-cropped, jet black hair, she was stunningly beautiful, poised, and articulate. Predictably, football player after player would try to seduce her. She politely rejected all advances. The next day these same men sat with mouths hanging open as she told them she was HIV positive.

"Some of you wanted to take me to bed last night," she'd begin in a room full of massive, muscular men who must have felt boyishly stupid. Once she had their attention, she told her story and educated them about HIV/AIDS.

Abstinence—The Only Sure HIV/AIDS Protection

Just a quarter of a century ago, hardly anyone in the United States had heard of human immunodeficiency virus/acquired immune deficiency syndrome (HIV/AIDS). First thought to be a disease confined to homosexuals, HIV today infects heterosexuals as well and is a pandemic claiming an estimated 36 million people worldwide.[2]

After nearly twenty years of living with this disease, the population now understands that HIV is transmitted by casual sex and not by casual contact. Blood transfusions—as was the case with tennis great Arthur Ashe, who received tainted blood during open-heart surgery—or shared needles similarly transmit this virus.

Former Lakers basketball hero Magic Johnson seems to be living well in spite of his diagnosis. Much of the credit goes to the new HIV "meds," a complicated series of chemotherapy that doctors began prescribing in 1996 that is criticized for causing nauseating side-effects. These drugs are allowing people with HIV/AIDS to live longer, but they do not guarantee a normal life span.

To protect the population, the Centers for Disease Control (CDC) recommends that the best protection against STDs including HIV/AIDS is abstinence or sexual intercourse with one mutually faithful, uninfected partner. Additionally, they recommend that condoms be made "widely available through health care providers who offer services to sexually active men and women, particularly in STD clinics, family planning clinics, and drug treatment centers."[3]

Recently the CDC has come under attack for intentionally misleading the public about the effectiveness of condoms in preventing devastating diseases such as AIDS and the Human papillomavirus (HPV) that can cause painful warts and/or cervical cancer.[4] Because of the CDC's false propaganda, millions of people rely on condoms as the solution to stopping the spread of sexually transmitted diseases. The result? Condoms are everywhere.

There is a movement afoot to infiltrate the church with the safer sex message. This movement is dangerous because it takes a little bit of truth and couches it in one big lie.

Balm in Gilead

Beware the Balm in Gilead! Billed as an organization that targets African-American churches to "exclusively build the capacity of Black churches to effectively address AIDS in their respective communities,"[5] its goal is to promote compromise and condoms. Statements that "most churches were in a state of denial and had confused their theological position on condoms and homosexuality with their Christian responsibility to address human suffering and the needs of their brothers and sisters as our Lord Jesus Christ taught," are distorted and intentionally manipulative.

Claiming to represent mainline denominations—a claim that deserves careful verification—Balm in Gilead suggests that the church has been "homophobic" and insensitive to people living with HIV/AIDS. Churches are exhorted to accept people as the Lord made them, which implies acceptance of unbiblical lifestyles under the guise of tolerance. This not-for-profit New York based organization does acknowledge the importance of the Black church in the community, which may explain why it is bankrolled by the Centers for Disease Control and other organizations that promote condoms as a primary means of HIV prevention. When considering whether or not to join Balm in Gilead, take care not to be deceived by spiritual-sounding cliches or feel defensive that *not* to join equals lack of compassion.

It is understandable that the world cannot comprehend that Christians can love the sinner but hate the sin. Since sinners do what sinners do—that is, sin—the nature of the sin doesn't matter, "for all have sinned and fall short of the glory of God" (Rom. 3:23). We do not want to confuse *sins*, the acts we commit in evidence that we are breaking the commandments, with *sin*, the state of men and women who do not have a personal relationship with God through Jesus Christ and who are therefore separated from God. The truth "that if you confess with your mouth, 'Jesus is Lord,' and believe in your heart that God raised him from the dead, you will be saved" (Rom. 10:9-10) applies to all. Equally applicable is 1 John 1:9-10: "If we confess our sins, [God] is faithful and just and will forgive us our sins and purify us from all unrighteousness. If we claim we have not sinned, we make him out to be a liar and his word has no place in our lives."

Acceptance of the sinner is not to be equated with accepting the sin. Any philosophy that suggests that believers' behaviors cannot conform with biblical standards denies the incarnational power of God. God's power will change lifestyle, because it is the same power that raised a dead Jesus from the grave.

That pastors cannot call sin what it is—sin—and still be politically correct has crippled some into falling into the arms of Balm in Gilead. Perhaps they believe that they must compromise and do something—*anything*—since so many people, especially in the black community, are contracting the AIDS virus. In their defense, perhaps these pastors are afraid of isolating the very people they are trying to win with the gospel. But careful reading of the Balm in Gilead website and materials uncovers a message of *acceptance* of homosexuality and nonmarital sexual activity. In other words, these lifestyles are subtly condoned, and worse, the message is that those who disagree do not love their brothers.

Beware the Form of Godliness

Balm in Gilead has a *form* of godliness. Outwardly and at first glance, it looks like religion. But when the covers are pulled back, it is evident that this message denies and rejects the true power of God to change minds and transform lives. The evidence is in the conduct Balm in Gilead recommends, conduct that ultimately rejects the uncompromising Word of God.

At a meeting where Balm in Gilead introduced their program to inner-city churches, there was no mistaking the agenda. Members in the audience questioned the de-emphasis of abstinence but were abruptly silenced.

"We tried abstinence. That doesn't work," was the retort. "Just preach messages of acceptance, get tested for HIV, and use latex condoms." A few pastors pulled out of the coalition once they understood the agenda of this group.

Church-Sensitive Curriculum

Another effort to "educate" the church is sponsored by the California Department of Health Services Office of AIDS that publishes curriculum they say is "church-sensitive."[6] Packaged in a striking navy blue and red binder, *Healing Begins Here: A Pastor's Guidebook for HIV/AIDS Ministry Through the Church* features the red AIDS ribbon superimposed over a cross that is suspended above open hands.

With Bible passages throughout, this curriculum discusses HIV/AIDS prevention, risky behavior, safer sex, and unprotected sex.[7] Pastors are told to inform their congregations to "practice safer sex, including using latex condoms correctly," and to "communicate with sexual partner(s) about ways to reduce risk." Pastors are also to instruct their members to "be aware of all sexual partners' risk behaviors (that is, sexual, drug use, etc.)."[8] They are to encourage everyone in their congregation to get tested for HIV and to teach that "the only way to eliminate your risk of getting HIV/AIDS and other STDs is to practice abstinence . . . . also properly using latex condoms can significantly reduce the risk of contracting HIV/AIDS."[9]

This is one of the two cursory mentions of abstinence in the ninety-six-page notebook. The second mention of abstinence is this: "Preach abstinence, teach prevention. HIV is a preventable disease that cannot be spread through casual contact."[10] It would have been biblical to suggest this instead: "Preach abstinence, period. HIV is a preventable disease that is primarily spread through casual sex."

The church historically has been the refuge where everyone—including homosexuals—has found forgiveness, acceptance, help, counsel, and spiritual healing. Pastors have no need to be defensive about preaching obedience to God's Word, whether the issue is lying, fornication, or homosexuality. God has already spoken.

> But mark this: There will be terrible times in the last days. People will be lovers of themselves, lovers of money, boastful, proud, abusive, disobedient to their parents, ungrateful, unholy, without love, unforgiving, slanderous, without self-control, brutal, not lovers of the good, treacherous, rash, conceited, lovers of pleasure rather than lovers of God—having a form of godliness but denying its power. Have nothing to do with them.
>
> 2 Timothy 3:1-5

Condoms in the Church?

Attempts to get churches to hand out condoms are not new. The First African Methodist Episcopal Church (FAME) in Los Angeles, with a 7,500-member congregation, distributed condoms to its members in 1991.[11]

Several other churches in LA received packages with condoms and lubricants in the mail but returned them.[12]

Inherent in this approach is the same presumption that has condoms in the schools: "Everybody's doing it." The argument goes that since HIV is deadly, abstinence may be the best prevention, but abstinence is not the only prevention.

Tragically, some of the pastors who distribute condoms may be sincere in their effort to save lives. But they are sincerely wrong to suggest that condoms are the best solution to HIV/AIDS prevention, to support condom distribution programs, or to be silent about handing out condoms in the church. Condoms are not what Christians are commanded to put on.

> The night is far spent, the day is at hand. Therefore let us cast off the works of darkness, and let us *put on the armor of light*. Let us walk properly, as in the day, not in revelry and drunkenness, not in lewdness and lust, not in strife and envy. But *put on the Lord Jesus Christ*, and make no provision for the flesh, to fulfill its lusts.
>
> Romans 13:12-14 NKJV (emphasis mine)

The word *provision* means "foreplanning, foresight, forethought, premeditated plan, making preparation for, providing for."[13] This passage cannot be applied to unbelievers; it is written to the church. We are not to plan in advance to sin. Recommending that parishioners abstain, but if they can't abstain use latex condoms, is confused double-talk that disregards this passage. God is not the author of confusion (1 Cor. 14:33). Using contraceptives to prevent pregnancy within the marital union is not morally wrong. But it is wrong to recommend the use of condoms to "encourage fornication and adultery, which are morally wrong."[14] This explanation from leading theologians in the field of ethics may offer further clarification:

> Using birth-control methods to treat sex casually and remove intimacy from the act does not alone make contraception morally wrong. Casual sex is most likely to occur when sex partners are not married to one another and are merely seeking their own pleasure. However, fornication and adultery are wrong not because one can use a birth-control device and thereby avoid genuine intimacy. They are wrong because God's Word prohibits them.[15]

Obedience is the Bible's ruler by which we evaluate our spiritual condition. There is a big difference between carnal, spiritual immature Christians and those who are unsaved. A true believer will repent and change his or her lifestyle.

God's message is clear. Preparing for sin by giving out condoms is not in the Christians' handbook, the Bible. Neither should it be an option presented in any other handbook used within the church. What should the church say with one unified voice?

Declaration on Sexual Morality

Focus on the Family, in conjunction with pastors and experts in the field, published a statement on sexual morality to assist pastors and churches. The Declaration on Sexual Morality overviews Old Testament and New Testament teachings to provide a cohesive statement on the Bible's teachings about sexuality. Social issues are also addressed.[16] Pastors and youth workers may find this resource valuable when confronted with alternatives like handing out condoms in the church (see appendix A).

Virginity Pledges

The church has been successful in teaching teenagers to abstain from sexual immorality primarily as a result of virginity pledges. Asking teens to vow to be sexually pure in the context of a seminar like *True Love Waits* is very effective. The message, pledge ceremony, and support of peers strengthens teens' commitment to chastity.

Happily, for those fighting the paper war, the track record for virginity pledges has been documented. A report by the Physicians Consortium, a network of nineteen state Physicians Resource Councils representing over two thousand physicians, summarized a study by Dr. Peter S. Bearman, director of the Institute for Social and Economic Research and Policy at Columbia University, and Dr. Hannah Brückner, assistant professor of sociology at Yale University. They examined data and the factors that reduce sexual risk-taking by teens from the National Longitudinal Study on Adolescent Health (AddHealth), the most extensive longitudinal research study of adolescent behavior.[17] Following are study highlights:

- Adolescents who take the virginity pledge are much less likely to have intercourse than adolescents who do not pledge.
- The delay effect is substantial and almost impossible to erase. Taking a pledge delays intercourse for a long time. . . . Pledging decreases the risk of intercourse substantially and independently.
- The pledge effect is strongly conditioned by age. Pledging does not work for adolescents at all ages. It works the most for younger adolescents.
- The pledge identity is induced and sustained through interacting with other pledgers in the community who make their pledge and commitment public. The pledge movement, in this sense, is an identity movement.[18]

The consortium adds this important comment:

As practicing physicians, we encounter the results of teenage sexual "experimentation" in the forms of unwed teenage parenthood, pregnancy scares, STDs and requests for abortion. Even many years later, the consequences can be as fatal as AIDS, as permanent as incurable herpes, and as heartbreaking as infertility.

> Our conclusion is that it is best for teens to refrain from sexual involvement until marriage. This is not only the best choice from a health perspective, but also for the purpose of a successful marriage. A delay to just a "later age" of sexual initiation is not a satisfactory target for us. Nevertheless, the pledge study research identified a delay in the median age of sexual initiation by pledgers, and this has important health implications.[19]

These doctors have spoken. Pastors and youth workers who present kids with the opportunity to take virginity pledges can be assured that statistically their efforts have a lasting effect. Here's why:

1. The pledge acknowledges that sexual activity is controllable.
2. The pledge places the locus of control upon the individual.
3. The pledge requires a conscious, purposeful decision, in contrast to the "if it happens, it happens" outlook of many teens.[20]

Not to be ignored in the pledge ceremony is the invitation for secondary virginity. Teens who have been sexually active can commit to a lifestyle of purity, and they do.

Strengthening the Pledge

Pledgers who do become sexually active do so at a significantly older age than non-pledgers. "Whatever the reason for this delay—the pledge itself, certain factors in the lives of pledgers, or a combination of the two—the fact remains that pledgers, as a group, experience first intercourse at an older age."[21] Delayed sexual activity is beneficial because teens who begin sex at an earlier age are at greater risk for STD infection including genital herpes, chlamydia, and HPV.

If some pledgers have sexual intercourse anyway, but at later ages, shouldn't they also be taught about condoms? "The Consortium recognizes that teens who abstain from sex need support to help them to continue to abstain until marriage, rather than having their resolve undermined by messages that may promote sexual activity."[22]

While the success of the pledge is wonderful news, why it works is admittedly complex. "Just getting a bunch of kids in a classroom to sign a pledge would ignore where the pledge gets its power. We believe that the pledge would be most effective when there is a supportive social structure. The vision for a successful marriage and family must be instilled by all components of society—parents, educators, youth workers, media, government and others."[23]

What else can the church do? As it continues to encourage families to worship together, the church contributes in a significant way to strong marriages and teen sexual purity.

Pray Together, Stay Together

The familiar adage—"The family that prays together stays together"—is actually anchored in solid statistics. Church attendance is the best predictor of marital stability. And, says Patrick F. Fagan of the Heritage Foundation, "Religion, by protecting marriages of parents, serves further to protect the virginity of their children."[24]

Here's how it works. Parents model their religious beliefs to their children who in turn develop a religious commitment of their own. Then, these children, because of their religious conviction, decide to abstain from non-marital sexual activity.

Research also shows that the religious worship of parents is directly linked to the sexual behavior of their children. "There is a very high connection between a father's religious practice and his children's virginity, slightly greater even than the strong connection between a mother's religious practice and her children's virginity," Fagan explains. "When both parents worship, this is magnified. There is a powerful, positive relationship to their children's sexual activity."[25]

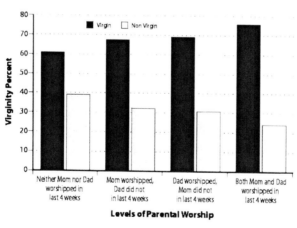

Parental Worship and Teen Virginity

Source: NLS Add Health   Calculations by Pat Fagan, The Heritage Foundation

Let's give the church a standing ovation! Church leaders are helping to make a difference. The last chapter includes more ways to involve pastors and youth workers in keeping kids sexually pure.

chapter 12

healing, hope, power

"Woman, where are they? Has no one condemned you?"
"No one, sir," she said.
"Then neither do I condemn you," Jesus declared.
"Go now and leave your life of sin."
John 8:10-11

Love and forgiveness, redemption and power, healing and hope are biblical themes that mirror the heart of the gospel. Jesus modeled for us what should be our response to sin and the sinner when he released the woman who was brought to him by an angry, accusing mob. She had been caught in the very act of adultery, and her rightful sentence was death by stoning. But Jesus did not condemn the woman. He forgave her and empowered her to leave her life of sin.

Jesus modeled to us the ministry of the church. We are to provide refuge for the hurting, the poor, the disenfranchised, the sick, and the sin-sick. Those of us who have been reclaimed from hell by the blood of Jesus Christ have been commissioned to do the work of the ministry. This is how "greater works" will be accomplished.

* * *

The parenting seminar was poorly attended. Out of a church of five thousand, only eight parents of children in the nursery, preschool, and kindergarten attended this workshop. Rather than focusing on who didn't attend, however, we gave our full attention to those who took time out on a Wednesday night to learn how to be better parents.

One young woman in particular caught my eye. She stomped into the room several steps ahead of her toddler son, who was trying in vain to catch up with her. Periodically she would stop and say, "Come on!" in an agitated voice. After taking him upstairs to the child care workers, she returned to join the class.

A series of exercises included small group discussion. Moms and dads shared their experiences and frustrations with the terrible twos, tantrums and all. With only a handful of parents, it was easy to monitor faces and weigh the impact of the material. "Yours too?" seemed to be the common question and similarly the shared relief. Suddenly parents did not feel so isolated in their experiences.

I watched the young lady who had walked so far ahead of her son. Slowly she relaxed when she heard that other children reacted just as her child did. During the course of the evening, we learned that the "sperm donor" for her child was not actively involved in parenting. This young lady was angry at him and angrier still at her circumstance. Most of the time she left her son to be raised by her mother, his grandmother.

At the end of the evening we gave group hugs, and that's when she broke down and cried. "I'm a terrible mother," she said to me. I watched the tears wash away anger and begin to cleanse her bitterness.

"No, you are a good mother!" I assured her.

"I'm not. I'm terrible."

"Look at how many people are here tonight," I continued. "Out of all of the people who attend our church, out of more than five thousand people, you're here. You came to learn how to be a better parent. You made the investment of time to learn how to raise your son. You're not a terrible mother. You're a *good* mother!"

A light went on. The woman's eyes widened. She understood. The next night I cried when I saw her walk into the classroom. She was walking with a smile, bouncing her little boy on her back.

* * *

Equipping parents in church-sponsored seminars is an excellent way to begin. Guest speakers may be parents, educators, or psychologists who have a vested interest in helping families.

Have a Positive Parenting Month

Devoting an entire month annually to parenting—Positive Parenting Month—underscores its importance. You might have class one evening every week and focus on a specific age group. How children develop and how to discipline head the list of information parents need to know.

Allow the adults time to share with one another, because sometimes they learn as much from shared experiences as they do from the instructors. Small group discussions interspersed throughout the presentation promote assurances that "you are not alone."

To make it easier for moms and dads to attend the sessions, arrange for child care for the little ones and homework assistance for older children. Limit the length of the sessions to one and a half hours in the evening so that parents get home at a reasonable time.

Start a MOPS Group

Churches should become involved in the lives of children as early as possible. Bonding with mothers by offering support and guidance in the child's early years is a way to let families know that churches care. Mothers of Preschoolers (MOPS), a nationwide ministry sponsored by Focus on the Family, provides the structure for mothers of young children to dialogue with and learn from other mothers.[1]

Minister to the Family

A pastor of family ministry can concentrate all of his or her efforts on the family. This might fall within the ministry of Christian Education, or it may be a separate entity. Designing Bible studies and classes, providing professional counseling services, being a resource for referral agencies, and networking with local social services are some suggestions for this vital position.

Emphasize Children's Ministry

Annual budgets reflect the church's priority when it comes to children's ministry. The emphasis in children's ministries flows from the top down, and it is the senior pastor who is ultimately responsible for casting the vision.

Children's Bible-centered curriculum should emphasize the importance of respect for and obedience to God. By fifth grade, children should be presented with opportunities to attend special seminars about sex. Be sure to screen presenters carefully and have signed permission slips from parents.

Train Teachers to Integrate Their Faith

Training Christian teachers how to integrate their faith with public school curricula is an important way to make the reality of the gospel come alive. Church-sponsored teacher-training workshops can give educators the confidence they need to effectively articulate their faith.[2] The Christian Educators Association International is an association of Christian teachers that helps with the issues teachers face in public schools.[3]

Provide Scholarships for Christian Teachers

As baby boomers reach retirement age, it is expected that 50 percent of today's teachers will retire from public schools in ten years. Why not replace these retirees by encouraging college students to teach? Churches can provide book or tuition scholarships to those who major in education.

Honor Teachers

One powerful suggestion for the church is to honor public and private school teachers in commissioning ceremonies at the start of each school year. This can be a special morning or evening service or can be incorporated in the regular worship hour. Ask teachers to come forward, and pray for them. Budget permitting, give them a token reminder—a bookmark or a card to post on their bulletin board—that the church is praying for them. Don't forget to honor that army of faithful volunteers who teach the children on Sunday mornings.

Support Christian Clubs

The best part of public schools is teachers who really care! Thankfully, some of these teachers lead on-campus Christian clubs.

The recent turmoil in high schools is evidence that children need to learn more than just how to spell and subtract. They need moral guidance. Christian clubs provide the balance that may be lacking in so many of these students' lives.

The explanation of the legal parameters for having Christian clubs on campus might help teachers, parents, and students start a Christian club in their school. According to public high school club faculty advisor, Jeff Eastridge, who teaches at Arroyo High School in El Monte, California, Christian clubs must be student-led. Usually, a certificated employee—a teacher—must be present at all meetings of student organizations. These faculty advisors assist with administrative tasks and ensure compliance with legal guidelines governing all student groups.

Legally, Christian clubs are to be permitted on public school campuses. This right was guaranteed with passage of the Equal Access Act, a right that has been upheld with cases such as *Westside Community Schools v. Mergens,* and *Lamb's Chapel v. Center Moriches Union Free School District.*[4]

Students who become members of campus Christian clubs come from various religious backgrounds with myriad beliefs and doctrines. Club members may be from the most liberal denominations or from the most ultraconservative churches. They may be cult members or even Buddhist or Muslim. Many students from nonchurched families view the club as their "church."

Faculty, staff, or other students who disagree with the Christian club's existence may present opposition. Ignorance of the law leads some to view these clubs as illegal and in violation of separation of church and state. Rather than being violations of the law, Christian clubs are protected by the law. Download "Knowing Your Rights: Students' Rights Legal Briefing" for more information[5] or contact the American Center for Law and Justice in Virginia.[6]

For a campus ministry to bear fruit, there must be a novel approach to outreach. Some parachurch organizations, such as the Fellowship of Christian Athletes, Young Life, and Youth for Christ are allowed on public school campuses, and they can assist the student leaders.[7]

Start Student-Led Bible Studies

Another recommendation from Eastridge is for churches to be actively engaged in training students to become small group leaders on their campuses. "Local ministries with a vision for outreach in public schools can identify and train spiritually mature student leaders in their congregation who have a heart for God and a teachable spirit. Training is important, because students usually select club officers by popularity and not necessarily spiritual gifting," says Eastridge.

According to Youth for Christ, close to 90 percent of those who become Christians do so before the end of their teenage years. The mission field is right under our noses! Christian teachers in public schools have an excellent opportunity to assist in life-changing ministry. Serving as club advisors not only helps students but also provides teachers with a "legal" outlet for expressing their faith.

Arrange Released Time

Released Time Bible Education is Christian education that occurs during regular school hours. Churches partner with public schools either directly or through affiliated independent organizations composed of church members to offer devotional Bible study off-campus as an elective during the school day.

Released Time is supported by the U.S. Constitution and affirmed by the Supreme Court.[8] For students to participate, parents must sign permission forms that allow their children to leave the campus during school hours to study Scripture. Schools can't initiate the program, and principals can't pressure students to attend. Schools and principals may, however, respond to requests from parents and churches or synagogues to release students during the day for religious education.

Isn't this a practical ministry for the church? There are usually several located in the neighborhood of a school with classrooms that often remain empty during the day. Inviting students to the church for Bible study often results in praise from teachers and administration who report marked differences in their students' attitudes and great improvement in the overall school climate.

With an abundance of printed curriculum in Christian bookstores, it is easy to find lessons that are right for the students in your community. Here's additional encouragement:

- 50-70% of youth entering this program are unchurched.
- Many attend with the hope of learning the biblical worldview to address issues in their lives.
- Released time increases the biblical knowledge of children who already attend church.
- Christian education assists parents, schools, and the community by reinforcing values that are key to wise decision-making.
- Students learn about the importance of prayer and become active in their schools to help spread the Gospel to other students.

Rather than complaining that Released Time takes students away from academic studies, teachers and administrators overwhelmingly agree that what really distracts from learning time are discipline problems and disrespect—issues that are minimized when students learn to respect God and therefore learn to respect themselves.[9] Drug involvement, violent behavior, and sexual promiscuity are changed when God's word and prayer become the focal point of students' daily education.

What an opportunity for the church! Trained teachers who make the Word of God come alive can help students understand how to read the Bible and how to apply it to their lives.[10] Some pastors report increased church attendance since parents want to connect with those who are positively influencing their children. Adults and children alike accepted Jesus Christ as their Savior. There is a national movement called the National Released Time Bible Education Project, which is designed to help Catholics, Evangelicals, and mainline Protestant churches develop viable programs in their churches. With 59 million students in grades K-12 and 30,000 churches for 100,000 public schools in the United States,[11] churches should not be content until every child is reached with the Gospel. For more information, contact School Ministries, Inc.[12]

Adopt a School

If every church intentionally prayed for the schools in their neighborhood, think about all of the children who would benefit. For more than ten years a janitor at one school prayed for that school as he walked the grounds. Today that campus boasts hundreds of Christians and an enormous Christian club that can be credited to the prayers that were diligently offered by that janitor. Check resources and organizations for more tips on how to pray for and how to care for public schools.[13]

In addition to prayer, provide mentors. School boards may welcome churches that provide mentors to "at-risk" kids.

Adopt a Teacher

Adopting a teacher means that the church will provide everything a teacher needs for his or her classroom. Budget shortages won't matter when members in the church are committed to providing supplies for their local school. Volunteers can help with organizing and cleaning up the classroom before or after the school year and may be available to assist throughout the term as needed.

Nurture Teachers

Start a ministry called Teachers Nurturing Teachers (TNT) in your church for all of the public school teachers who attend. They can meet once a month or more with the goal of supporting, networking, sharing information, and praying for one another. For those who may be the only Christian teacher in the school, it helps to know they are not alone.

Prepare Kids

Prepare kids so that when they walk into a classroom, they know how to handle some of the issues with which they are confronted. The National Network of Youth Ministries in San Diego is doing a lot of work in this area, equipping youth pastors and students in public schools. Their mission is to expose every teenager to the Gospel of Jesus Christ, establish those who respond in local churches, and disciple them to reach the world. Youth for Christ also sponsors an evangelism training conference, DC/LA, that helps middle and high school kids tell God's story and their own.[14] Needed is a similar high-powered conference specifically tailored and priced to reach the urban poor.

Provide After-School Programs

Churches that provide after-school care may be eligible for funds to support this ministry to the family. This is a great opportunity for outreach into the community. Parents trust the church, and having tutors on hand, feeding the children, and scheduling time for recreation will give kids the supervision they deserve. There are state and federal funds available for ministries that provide recreation and supervision. Faith teaching would have to be provided for with separate funding, or invite a church staff member to rotate from room to room and talk with each group of kids.

Train Tutors

Provide trained tutors to volunteer to help students after school, and offer tutoring at church or at school at least one night a week. This is another way churches can meaningfully impact the lives of the children. Churches may receive state or federal support for tutoring too. Again, any faith teaching must be provided for under a separate budget. As with after-school care, tutors may invite church staff to talk to kids.

Train Youth Pastors

Training the men and women who in turn teach and disciple the kids in your church is key. Invest in them by sponsoring them to be trained, equipped, and encouraged. The guarantee is that staff will return to your church ready to teach and disciple kids in new effective ways.

Youth Specialties sponsors training seminars and conventions to equip youth pastors so they get on track and stay on track.[15] The Urban Youth

Workers Institute offers weekend training for youth leaders and volunteers who minister in urban settings.[16]

Open a Youth Center

With parents who work, many kids are left with little to no supervision once school is out. Churches that provide recreational facilities—youth centers—demonstrate that they really *do* care about families.

Crenshaw Christian Center in Inglewood, California, where Dr. Frederick K. C. Price is the founder and pastor, is one of the largest and most prominent African-American churches in the country. Their sprawling campus, home of the Faith Dome, has one of the most impressive buildings ever that's designed just for teens—the Billy Blank Youth Activity Center.

Imagine, a building solely dedicated to youth! Churches that are financially able would do well to follow the lead of this trend-setting ministry. By providing a quality gymnasium along with supervised activities on evenings and weekends, this church offers a real alternative for kids who have too much free time. It's an excellent example of the church being the church and contributing to the community in a tangible way.[17]

Partner with the Roman Catholic Church

The Roman Catholic Church has been unprecedented in its stance on moral issues such as abortion and the right to life. Often they have stood alone. There is strength in numbers, so partnering with other congregations can provide alliances for networking and information sharing. Why not engage in a joint effort to educate the congregation and adopt the Catholic Church's resolve to be outspoken about issues affecting the community?

Develop an HIV/AIDS Ministry

People living with HIV/AIDS need the church, so developing an HIV/AIDS ministry is a must. Many have found refuge and comfort, but much more needs to be done. Consider having support groups and trained volunteers who can provide services to the sick and shut-in, such as cooking and cleaning. Additional ministries include HIV/AIDS education, counseling, legal advice, financial support, and medical assistance.

Churches can also provide hospice care by designating a home to be used for those who are too ill to care for themselves. An outreach ministry could be developed to reach unchurched HIV/AIDS sufferers. Recruiting workers from an HIV support group might be one way to provide meaningful employment.

Educate the congregation and enlist them to donate money, clothes, supplies, and time. Rocking AIDS babies in hospitals and providing homes for these children are other ways to put the gospel into action.

Open or Support a Crisis Pregnancy Center

Crisis pregnancy centers make a practical, loving effort to help women avoid aborting their babies. They function in three areas: intervention, prevention, and reconciliation. Providing pregnancy tests and supplying necessities such as clothing and furniture are ways that churches can intervene in the life of frightened mothers-to-be.

They also offer classes to provide reconciliation for anyone who has already had an abortion and needs to know the reality of God's forgiveness in her life. Funding may be available to start such a ministry.[18]

Rely on Professional Counselors

Know the law when it comes to the children in your care, and rely on professional counselors in cases of sexual assault or any form of abuse. Pastors, youth workers, and teachers who suspect there may be abuse or who learn of any instance of abuse *must* report it to the police *immediately*. Leaders who are ignorant of the law may endanger children and jeopardize families, as was the case in this following true account. Check with the local police department and with the office of social services in your community.

* * *

Susan (not her real name) is the mother of two children, an eight-year-old daughter and a ten-year-old son. Separated from her husband, she is raising her children alone. Because she works in a campus setting in Anywhere, U.S.A., Susan was fortunate to be able to bring her children to work with her.

Susan's safe haven began to crumble the day she learned that her daughter had been touched by a man who lived on campus. She went to her pastor for counseling, and he talked and prayed with her.

Two weeks later, both children were missing. Susan panicked and called the police. They arrived promptly, accompanied by a female officer trained in sexual assault. By the time the police arrived, the children surfaced. They had been playing "hide and seek." Unwilling to take any chances, the police asked questions to find out if someone had taken them away and then decided to bring them back. "No," both children affirmed.

Then the female police officer took the daughter aside and in her skilled way asked if anyone had ever touched her. The child said yes and told what had happened weeks earlier. Immediately both children were taken from their mother by the police into protective custody and placed in a foster home. Because Susan had not reported the sexual assault to the police but had confided in her pastor instead, she was accused of endangering her children.

The man who assaulted the child was arrested and then released for lack of evidence. The children, however, remain in foster care. Susan, who is only permitted supervised one-hour visits, must take state-mandated parenting and sexual abuse classes before she can have her children back at home.

* * *

How different might this scenario have been had this woman's pastor made one phone call! Pastors may feel they have settled the issue with God through counseling and prayer, but they have missed the first legal step.

Immediate reporting of sexual or physical abuse is designed to protect children. Evaluating the situation, the severity of the abuse, and the potential danger in which the child remains are to be determined by professionals. Here is the policy: All *suspected* cases of sexual or physical abuse must be reported to the proper authorities *immediately*. Failure to do so is nothing less than being irresponsible. The person who first learns of the abuse is the one who should make the phone call immediately. Don't wait for the "proper" church authority to make the report. The child remains in danger, and if too much time passes, it may be too late.

Know the policy. Teach the policy. And post the policy in clear view of all who are assigned to work with children.

Fingerprint Volunteers

Protecting children means that all church volunteers are fingerprinted before they are allowed in the classroom. A live scan fingerprint goes from the police department, where it is taken by computer to the Department of Justice via that same computer. The Department of Justice will return the results and state whether the person has been cleared.

A thorough application process includes background checks by calling references, conducting personal interviews, and constantly supervising all new personnel. The two-by-two rule that every teacher must be accompanied by another adult and that no teacher or youth worker is to be alone with a child provides protection for both the children and the church. For more information on how churches can provide a safe environment, contact Church Risk Management.[19]

Train Peer Models

As documented earlier, church attendance is a consistent variable among students who affirm abstinence. To maximize abstinence education, the church can train teenagers to volunteer as peer models in their high schools. Peer models seek opportunities to discuss abstinence with their friends and are prepared to be advocates of abstinence in their classes when appropriate, such as during presentations or debates. Teenage peer models who go through this training and remain abstinent might earn college scholarships to be awarded by the churches they attend.

Institute Rites of Passage

Although traditionally "African" in heritage, all boys might benefit from rites of passage training that is spearheaded by the men in the church.[20] Within this context, teenage males can learn responsibility for themselves and for their community through structured holistic curriculum that encompasses the spiritual, the educational, the relational, and the vocational.

For these young men, manhood would be redefined from sexual conquests to social responsibility. The communal value of accountability to one another, as well as to the leaders, must be emphasized. Such training is, of course, based on biblical values.

Open Church Schools

Churches can open alternative schools for elementary, middle, and high school students. Support from the congregation along with modest tuition fees may be ways to underwrite most of the school's expenses. The Association of Christian Schools International (see *www.acsi.org*) provides information and guidelines.

* * *

Bravo to churches that are already doing any of the above! Around the country, there are probably hundreds of additional ways being implemented to assist families and build better communities.

Remember that in *Keeping Your Kids Sexually Pure*, the word "keeping" implies an ongoing process. It involves all of us. And it begins with us. Parents, pastors, youth workers, and teachers are role models who leave lasting impressions. As Paul admonished Timothy in 1 Timothy 4:12, we are to "set an example for the believers in speech, in life, in love, in faith and in purity."

As I draw to a close, I want to share a message gleaned from a recent personal experience.

* * *

Earlier this week I had a dream that I was telling someone how vital studying the book of Romans was for living a holy life. When I awoke, I chuckled to myself, because I love Romans. Study of the great doctrines outlined in this letter by the apostle Paul is foundational for understanding why and how to live victoriously.

Yesterday I visited a church that just completed a massive building campaign. Members of the West Angeles Church of God in Christ in Los Angeles are celebrating in their stunning new cathedral, and I wanted to see the finished product. This past Sunday seemed like a great day to visit and satisfy my curiosity.

Before the message, an oppressive spirit seemed to be hovering in the air. The service dragged on heavily, and it even crossed my mind to leave. When Bishop Blake announced that he felt exhausted and then plopped into his seat as the choir sang a final song before his message, I had no idea we were in the midst of spiritual warfare.

It wasn't until this pastor struggled to begin his sermon that I realized what was occurring. His audible plea, "Please, God, help me preach this message!" ignited intercessors everywhere. I could feel that oppressive spirit lift, and it soon became obvious why the enemy had tried to hinder him.

When the bishop asked the congregation to turn to the book of Romans, I leaned forward in my seat—Romans, the book I love, about which I had just dreamed. Suddenly I realized that it was not curiosity that had drawn me here. God had indeed navigated my steps.

The message, "Shall We Continue in Sin?" was based on Romans 6:1. What a powerful word from God! I understood why I was sitting in this church on this particular Sunday morning, having just "completed" (or so I thought) the final chapter to the book you are now reading. Although I was finished writing, God wasn't.

"Shall We Continue in Sin?" was an exhortation that was not just meant for the West Angeles congregation. I believe it was a question to be posed to a larger body of believers—the readers of this book. (See Appendix B for the text of Bishop Blake's sermon.)

Here is a question for the church, God's people, born-again, blood-bought believers. It is not intended for anyone who has not been born again according to John 3:3 and Romans 10:9-10. Paul is writing to *Christians*, and his call to abandon a lifestyle of sin is directed to the *church*.

Shall we continue in sin? Why is such a question even necessary? From the pulpit to the pew, we must examine ourselves. As Christians, we do not need to point a finger at the world, because sinners are doing what they are supposed to do—sin. We need only look at ourselves and take the beams out of our own eyes.

There are several reasons why there is sexual sin in the church. Heading the list is pride, which has led too many men in leadership to flirt on a dangerous precipice.

> You, then, who teach others, do you not teach yourself? You who preach against stealing, do you steal? You who say that people should not commit adultery, do you commit adultery? You who abhor idols, do you rob temples?
>
> Romans 2:21-22

The lust of the eye, the lust of the flesh, and the pride of life are still great pitfalls. Unfortunately, some pastors have lost their passion for ministry, but they persist in their "jobs" because their livelihood is wrapped in Sunday morning offerings. As a result, ministry to the body becomes the lowest priority, and the Bible is not taught with fervor and urgency as it once was.

Couched in this apathy are seared consciences and lax lifestyles. Making money seems to be more important than making disciples. Ultimately afraid to offend and lose members, truth trickles from the pulpit in watered-down versions. Impotent church leaders tolerate the intolerable, pretending not to notice the obvious. Of course, this is not everyone. But if the shoe fits, it may be because it's on that pastor's foot!

> Nevertheless, the firm foundation of God stands, having this seal, "The Lord knows those who are His," and "Let everyone who names the name of the Lord abstain from wickedness."
>
> 2 Timothy 2:19 NASB

In too many congregations, silly women allow creeps to creep into their homes.

> For of this sort are they which creep into houses, and lead captive silly women laden with sins, led away with divers lusts, ever learning, and never able to come to the knowledge of the truth.
>
> 2 Timothy 3:6-7 KJV

Such women fall for any line as long as *he* carries a Bible. In desperation they toss aside God's standards hoping that something right—marriage—will result from something wrong—a defiled bed. They get hurt, "learn" their lesson, only to repeat the same cycle with the next smooth-talking preacher. No wonder the Bible calls such weak-willed women "silly"!

"Shall we continue in sin?" is also a question for the people in the pews. The divorce rate of couples in the church is the same as that of couples in the world. How can this be when we have the power of God in our lives and faith in his Word? Or do we? And what about the children?

If the church would right itself, the ripple effect would echo into the world. May God open our ears and eyes with this warning. (See appendix B for the text of Bishop Blake's sermon.)

As pastors and youth workers continue to preach and teach, they should revisit the book of Romans often. Furthermore, if all Christians would complete a class in Romans, they would be better equipped to live the Christian life as God intended.

* * *

The challenge for the church of Jesus Christ to be sexually pure is great. After all, we are the salt of the earth and lights on a hill. May God forgive us for the times we have failed him and then bless us to do his will in the earth. And may we have the wisdom to keep our kids sexually pure as we remember that sexual purity begins with us.

postscript

La Nelle, my twenty-year-old niece, attends a local Christian college and was staying with Irving and me during her summer break. We had almost forgotten what it was like having a young person around the home—just past teenager/not quite adult, too old to assign chores to/too young not to.

The most challenging task, we had thought, was encouraging La Nelle to resist the urge to relax in front of the television set. Once she secured a summer job, we breathed a sigh of relief. That is, until the dating began. He was just a friend, we were told, but they went to the movies and stayed out past midnight. Irving waited up. I tried unsuccessfully to sleep, but finally got up, dressed, put on a little makeup, and joined the vigil.

The young man dropped La Nelle off a little after 1 A.M. When I heard the car, I went outside and asked him to please come in. Since we were not home when they had left (after work, Irving and I went to exercise at a nearby park and didn't get back until after 8:30), we had not met this young man face-to-face. So what better time for "the interview" than now?

Irving asked questions about family, school, job, and career. I asked if he had a personal relationship with Jesus Christ and if he was committed to sexual purity. When he affirmed yes to both questions, we explained that this was our expectation for our niece. After about a solid half hour eye-to-eye, the interview ended, and he was on his way. Later I learned what he said to La Nelle as she walked him to his car. "What did you tell them? I thought we were *just* friends!" "We are. It doesn't matter, though. That's just the way they are," she said. "You mean you have to go through this *every* time you go out?" "Yep. They love me."

declaration on sexual morality

(Abridged Statement)

The Bible reveals that God's character defines for us what it means to be sexually pure: God's mandate to His people is to "be holy, because I am holy."[1]

We believe that God intends for people to enjoy sex within His established limits. However, because we live in a fallen world, we also believe the following:

Desire and experience cannot be trusted to set the morality of sex.[2] The morality of sex is set by God's holiness.[3]

God's standard is purity in every thought about sex, as well as in every act of sex. Sexual purity is violated even in thoughts that never proceed to outward acts.[4] Sex must never be used to oppress, wrong or take advantage of anyone.[5] Rape, incest, sexual abuse, pedophilia, voyeurism, prostitution and pornography always exploit and corrupt.[6]

God's standards for sexual moral purity protect human happiness.[7] But sex is not an entitlement, nor is it needed for personal wholeness or emotional maturity.

God calls some to a life of marriage and others to lifelong celibacy, but His calling to either state is a divine gift worthy of honor and respect.[8] No one is morally compromised by following God's call to either state, and no one can justify opposing a divine call to either state by denying the moral goodness of that state.

Sexual behavior is moral only within the institution of heterosexual, monogamous marriage. Marriage is secure only when established by an unconditional, covenantal commitment to *lifelong fidelity,*[9] and we should not separate what God has joined.[10] However, the Bible does discuss limited grounds that *may* justify divorce.[11]

Marriage protects the transcendent significance of personal sexual intimacy. Heterosexual union in marriage expresses the same sort of holy, exclusive, permanent, complex, selfless and complementary intimacy that some day will characterize the union of Christ with the redeemed and glorified Church.[12]

Sex in marriage should be an act of love and grace that transcends the petty sins of human selfishness and should be set aside only when both partners agree to do so, and then only for a limited time of concentrated prayer.[13]

Sex outside of marriage is never moral.[14] This includes all forms of intimate sexual stimulation that stir up sexual passion between unmarried partners.[15] Such behavior offends God[16] and often causes physical and emotional pain and loss in this life.[17] Refusal to repent of sexual sin may indicate that a person never has entered into a saving relationship with Jesus Christ.[18]

The Old and New Testaments uniformly condemn sexual contact between persons of the same sex;[19] and God has decreed that no one can ever excuse homosexual behavior by blaming his or her Creator.[20]

The moral corruption of sexual sin can be fully forgiven through repentance and faith in Christ's atonement,[21] but physical and emotional scars caused by sexual sin cannot always be erased in this life.[22]

Christians must grieve with and help those who suffer hardship caused by sexual immorality, even when it is caused by their own acts of sin.[23] But we must give aid in ways that do not deny moral responsibility for sexual behavior.[24]

We want to help men and women understand God's good plan for sexual conduct, and thereby to realize all the joy, satisfaction and honor God offers to sexual creatures made in His image.

I have read the ***Colorado Statement on Biblical Sexual Behavior*** and I agree with it. My signature below signifies my public endorsement of the *Colorado Statement. Focus on the Family* has my permission to publish my name in a list of endorsers.

Name: _____

Church/organization: _____

Address: _____

Signature: _____

Authors

Daniel Heimbach, Ph.D., is leader of the Declaration team and is professor of Christian ethics at Southeastern Baptist Seminary. He served as associate director for Domestic Policy and deputy executive secretary of the Domestic Policy Council in the George H. W. Bush administration. Dr. Heimbach also served as deputy assistant secretary of the Navy for Manpower. A board member with the Council on Biblical Manhood and Womanhood, Dr. Heimbach has written extensively on the Bible's teaching on human sexual behavior.

Craig L. Blomberg, Ph.D., is professor of New Testament at Denver Seminary and is regarded as one of the nation's foremost authorities on the Gospels. He was the primary author of a previous Focus booklet titled "What the Bible Really Says About Sex," which was a response to a booklet written by Debra Haffner of the Sex Information and Education Council of the United States (SIECUS).

Wayne Strickland, Ph.D., is professor of theology and academic dean at Multnomah Bible College and former regional chair of the Evangelical Theological Society. Dr. Strickland's dissertation was on Paul's use of "natural" and "unnatural" in Romans 1.

Peter Jones, Ph.D., is chairman of the Biblical Studies Department at Westminster Seminary (California Campus). He is also a board member of the Council on Biblical Manhood and Womanhood.

Daniel Juster, Ph.D., is president of Tikkun Ministries, an organization that oversees and helps dozens of Messianic congregations throughout the country and that also oversees several Messianic missions organizations. Dr. Juster is one of the most highly respected men in the Messianic movement.

Father Francis Martin, Ph.D., of the John Paul II Institute for Studies on Marriage and Family has written extensively on the topics of marriage, family, and sexuality.

La Verne Tolbert, Ph.D., has twenty-five years experience in the field of abstinence education. She has written curriculum on abstinence for A. C. Green and character education curriculum for inner-city children for the Medical Institute for Sexual Health. Her dissertation examined students' perceptions about condom availability and school-based clinics.

Steven R. Tracy, Ph.D., is professor of theology and ethics and vice president of Academic Affairs at Phoenix Seminary. Dr. Tracy's specialty is sexual ethics.

Rev. Roy A. Holmes is senior pastor of the Greater Walters A.M.E. Zion Church in Chicago.

shall we go on sinning?

A Message by Bishop Charles E. Blake[1]

As Christians, we need to ask ourselves, shall we continue in sin? Shall we go on sinning? That's the same question Paul asked the church at Rome: "What shall we say, then? Shall we go on sinning so that grace may increase? By no means! We died to sin; how can we live in it any longer?" (Rom. 6:1).

Earlier, Paul declared his faith in the gospel and commitment to God's purpose—to reveal and to establish his righteousness throughout his kingdom. "I am not ashamed of the gospel, because it is the power of God for the salvation of everyone who believes: first for the Jew, then for the Gentile. For in the gospel a righteousness from God is revealed, a righteousness that is by faith from first to last, just as it is written: 'The righteous will live by faith'" (Rom. 1:16-17).

Righteousness, or right acting, is in contrast to wickedness, the cause of God's displeasure, anger, and intense wrath. "The wrath of God is being revealed from heaven against all the godlessness and wickedness of men" (Rom. 1:18). "Godlessness" is a lack of love and a lack of desire for God. If you don't have an interest in pleasing God and doing the will of God, then you're living a godless life. "Wickedness" is an inclination toward the things that are wrong and sinful. Romans 3:23 tells us, "For all have sinned and fall short of the glory of God."

Another Representative

Since we failed through our representative, Adam, we lost the wonderful glory and fellowship of our first state. We all have sinned. But God provided another representative, Jesus Christ, the Son of God, to restore us to our former place in God.

God did not say "Get rid of your sin, get righteous, get good, and then I will send my Son to die for you." God did not wait until we were worthy or until we were righteous, because we could not have done it by ourselves.

> At just the right time, when we were still powerless, Christ died for the ungodly. Very rarely will anyone die for a righteous man, though for a good man someone might possibly dare to die. But God demonstrates his own love for us in this: While we were still sinners, Christ died for us.
>
> Romans 5:6-8

Imagine dying for us while we were enemies of God! God knew that we would be involved in that which was nauseating and irritating to him. But Jesus took our hands and God's hands and placed them together. He *reconciled* us to God. Because of Christ's resurrection, our lives are enhanced through the great gift of salvation.

> Since we have now been justified by his blood, how much more shall we be saved from God's wrath through him! For if, when we were God's enemies, we were reconciled to him through the death of his Son, how much more, having been reconciled, shall we be saved through his life!
>
> Romans 5:9-10

In other words, we rejoice and we have joy in our hearts because we have been brought back together with God through Jesus Christ. "Not only is this so, but we also rejoice in God through our Lord Jesus Christ, through whom we have now received reconciliation" (Rom. 5:11). Through Jesus Christ, we bring adequate glory to God. The glory of God is magnified when we recognize him, worship him, serve him, and live righteously before him.

Child of God, if you are saved, you have something to be thankful for. Because though you were alienated from God because of your sin, through Jesus Christ you were brought into oneness with God, and it was all done by the grace of God. "Therefore, since we have been justified through faith, we have peace with God through our Lord Jesus Christ, through whom we have gained access by faith into this grace in which we now stand" (Rom. 5:1-2). Standing is taken from the same root word that stability is taken from. And it really means that we have stability in God. We have a solid position, a standing place, by faith through the grace of God in the salvation that the Lord has given unto us.

Grace to Sin?

Paul knew that there would be some who would say, "Since we are saved by grace, we can do anything we want to do. Since God has put us in this solid position, since God loves us so much, and since Jesus had to save us anyway, then it doesn't make any difference how we live. We can live any way we want to live." Paul confronted this twisted rationale: "Shall we go on sinning so that grace may increase?" (Rom. 6:1).

He answered this rhetorical question by saying, "By no means!" Absolutely not! God forbid! No way! There's no way that we should continue sinning just because we have received the grace of God.

Why? To continue in sin would thwart God's purpose in sending his Son to the cross in the first place. It would thwart the purpose of the gospel, which is to reveal the righteousness of God. If God's people continue to sin and to live wickedly, then this is contrary to the very plan that God has always had for his kingdom. Those who associate themselves with God must associate themselves with God's purposes and with his objectives—righteousness.

God has done everything for us. He has given his Son for us that we might have life, and that more abundantly (John 10:10). His Son gave his life. Therefore we ought to be about doing the will of God. *God give me strength to preach this message today!*

> For the grace of God that brings salvation has appeared to all men. It teaches us to say "No" to ungodliness and worldly passions, and to live self-controlled, upright and godly lives in this present age, while we wait for the blessed hope—the glorious appearing of our great God and Savior, Jesus Christ, who gave himself for us to redeem us from all wickedness and to purify for himself a people that are his very own, eager to do what is good.
>
> Titus 2:11-14

God wants you to be excited about doing good. Jesus came to help us deny ungodliness and worldly lusts and live soberly, righteously, and godly in this present age.

Seven Ways

When you continue in sin, there are seven ways that you foil the very purpose of God for your life.

1. *When you continue in sin, you befriend the same sin that caused Jesus to be crucified.* This does not make God the Father very happy. Several years ago, my son was brutally shot in the doorway of his home. If I had seen you walking with your arms around the man who shot him, I would have been very unhappy with you. It was sin that caused Jesus to forsake the divine glory of heaven and come down to this earth. It was sin that caused him to be hung on the cross. It was sin that caused his untold agony. And when you as a believer become involved in sin, you wrap your arms around the very thing that caused Jesus to die in the first place.

2. *When you continue in sin, you squander the investment that God has made in your life.* What if I worked, struggled, and strategized to give you five thousand dollars to help you get through an ordeal, knowing that this investment was going to transform your life and put you back on your feet and pull you out of a pitiful environment? If you took the money and threw it into the ocean, you would be squandering my investment. God has invested the Old Testament, the prophets, the law, the sacrifices, the psalms of David, his only begotten Son, all of the apostles, all of the biblical writers, and all of the preachers of the gospel. God has made a great investment in you that you might live righteously.

3. *When you continue in sin, you expose yourself to the consequences of your action.* Sin is destructive. Most of the problems in your life are because of sin. Most of the animosity, most of the trouble, most of the distress, most of the conflict has taken place because of sin. You are no superperson. When I was a little boy I watched too much of the program *Superman,* and I decided that I too would fly. I went down to the playground with a little towel around my neck and got onto a swing and started swinging. At the optimum height, I let go, and for a minute I was just soaring. And then in another minute, I saw stars everywhere! I had made a one-point landing on the ground right on my chin, and I haven't tried to fly anymore, because I'm just like everyone else. You are just like everyone else. No one can take sin to his breast and walk away untouched, unstained, and undamaged. When you continue in sin, you join with that which will destroy you. And as I said, you're just like everybody else. If it hurt others, it's going to hurt you. What makes you think that you're so wonderful that you're going to get away when so many others who were smarter than you were destroyed?

4. *When you continue in sin, you go defenseless into the devil's territory.* You need a defense to live on this earth. You need God's help and protection to survive on this earth. But when you continue in sin you lose God's protection, because you leave God's direction and are on the devil's territory. The devil has every right to go to God and say, "You see, they've left you. They're on my territory now. You should not stop me from bringing my destruction down upon them, because if they had wanted your protection, they would have stayed under your direction." First Peter 5:8 says, "Be self-controlled and alert. Your enemy the devil prowls around like a roaring lion looking for someone to devour."

5. *When you continue in sin, you lose favor and fellowship with God.* When you get on the devil's territory, you lose the favor and the blessing and the power of almighty God. Romans 11:20-22 says, "Do not be arrogant, but be afraid. For if God did not spare the natural branches, he will not spare you either. Consider therefore the kindness and sternness of God: sternness to those who fell, but kindness to you, provided that you continue in his kindness. Otherwise, you also will be cut off." Now Paul was writing to saved folk, and he said that if he didn't spare the Jews when they refused to accept Christ and refused to conform to God's law but cut them off and grafted you in, don't you know that if you are grafted, and he cut the natural branches off, that he will cut you off? When God saves you, you need to keep on reaching out for God and stay in God's will. You need to get in the Word and study the Word and conform your life to the will of God.

6. *When you continue in sin, you join forces with the enemy and you contribute negatively to sin's destructive impact in the world.* Jesus died to bring righteousness, and here you are, a believer, introducing sin and wickedness into the world! Jesus died to help us do right, and here you are a child of God doing wrong, involved in this and involved in that.

> Don't you know that when you offer yourselves to someone to obey him as slaves, you are slaves to the one whom you obey—whether you are slaves to sin, which leads to death, or to obedience, which leads to righteousness?
>
> Romans 6:16

If you are obeying the devil, you are serving the devil. If you are obeying God, you are serving God.

7. *When you continue in sin, you face the judgment of God.*

If we deliberately keep on sinning after we have received the
knowledge of the truth, no sacrifice for sins is left, but only a fearful
expectation of judgment and of raging fire that will consume the
enemies of God. Anyone who rejected the law of Moses died without
mercy on the testimony of two or three witnesses. How much more
severely do you think a man deserves to be punished who has trampled
the Son of God under foot, who has treated as an unholy thing the
blood of the covenant that sanctified him, and who has insulted the
Spirit of grace? For we know him who said, "It is mine to avenge; I will
repay," and again, "The Lord will judge his people." It is a dreadful
thing to fall into the hands of the living God.

Hebrews 10:26-31

God already gave his Son to die for our sins. He is not going to issue
another plan of salvation. Once you neglect this great salvation and continue
in sin, all that awaits you is a fearful expectation of certain judgment and
fiery indignation.

You see, there is a line somewhere. Most try to stay as close to that line
as they possibly can get. "Is it all right for me to do this? Can I still be saved
and go there? Is it wrong to do this? Will the Lord accept it if I do the other
thing?" The real questions they are asking are these: "How much can I do
and still be saved? How close to the devil can I get and still be in God? How
close to sin can I get and still be in the will of God?"

They should be asking, "How far away from sin can I get? How far away
from the devil can I run? How close can I get to the Lord?" Listen, when
the Lord Jesus comes into your life, you ought not to be looking for God's
minimum standards. You ought to be striving and praying to go as high in God
as you can possibly go and get to know as much of God as you can possibly
know. As the old hymn says,

My heart has no desire to stay
Where doubts arise and fears dismay.
Tho' some may stay where these abound,
My prayer, my aim is higher ground.

I'm pressing on the upward way,
New heights I'm gaining ev'ry day.
Still praying as I'm upward bound,
"Lord, plant my feet on higher ground."

171

Since we don't know where that line is, we need to get as far away from that line and as close to God as we can get. Child of God, your blessing is in getting close to God.

Conclusion

Romans 6:5 says, "If we have been united with him like this in his death, we will certainly also be united with him in his resurrection." Jesus died in our place that our sins might be forgiven. And so we're forgiven, and we're justified. When you come to God and say, "Lord, in Jesus' name, I'm sorry for all of my sins. I believe on the Lord Jesus. I believe that he is the Son of God. I believe that he died for my sins. I believe that he rose from the dead," all of your sins are forgiven, and you are justified.

"Justified" means that you stand before God as if you have never committed a sin in all of your life, as if you have never sinned before. You become just as righteous as Jesus. Because you are like him in his death, you'll be like him in his resurrection. His resurrection body was a different kind of body. His first body died, but his second body was never to die again. He stood in that resurrection body and said: "Do not be afraid. I am the First and the Last. I am the Living One; I was dead, and behold I am alive for ever and ever! And I hold the keys of death and Hades" (Rev. 1:17-18).

We are going to be like him in his resurrection! So when you come to God, and you receive the Lord's forgiveness, the Lord works the wonder of regeneration in your life. He imparts to you a new nature. In baptism, you are buried beneath the water to symbolize the death of Jesus Christ. Your old nature is dead.

> In the same way, count yourselves dead to sin but alive to God in Christ Jesus. Therefore do not let sin reign in your mortal body so that you obey its evil desires. Do not offer the parts of your body to sin, as instruments of wickedness, but rather offer yourselves to God, as those who have been brought from death to life; and offer the parts of your body to him as instruments of righteousness.
> Romans 6:11-13

When you accept Jesus, the old man of sin loses his authority. He is buried in death with Jesus Christ. If a criminal committed a terrible crime and was sentenced to die, and if by some miracle he comes back to life again, he would never go back and do the very sin that caused him to be killed in the first place. He would walk in righteousness, and he would avoid that sin for the rest of his life.

Child of God, Jesus died for the sins that you have committed, and he paid the price for your sin. It is paid in full, and you are free, never to be condemned again.

> Therefore, there is now no condemnation for those who are in Christ Jesus, because through Christ Jesus the law of the Spirit of life set me free from the law of sin and death.
>
> Romans 8:1-2

When he rose again, you rose again with him, and you rose again *in* him and live in him.

It's just like going to the airport. You can't fly on your own. You can't go 30,000 feet and you can't go 600 miles an hour. But you get *in* the airplane. And the airplane does the rest. It goes down the runway. It takes off into the air. It goes up to 30,000 feet at 600 miles an hour. In a little while, you're walking around in an altogether different city telling people, "I flew in just a few moments ago."

No, *you* didn't fly in! The plane flew in, but you were *in* the plane. That's the secret. You can't live righteously. You can't avoid sin. You can't obey the law of God. But when you get *in* Christ—Christ in you, the hope of glory—he gives you a new nature.

> Therefore, if anyone is in Christ, he is a new creation; the old has gone, the new has come!
>
> 2 Corinthians 5:17

To walk in the way of God, you must get in Christ. The reason you can't live right is because you are walking after the flesh. You are trying to please the flesh. You have lost your spiritual vision. You are looking at the here and the now. But there is more than the here and the now. There is more than this flesh in which you live.

"God is spirit, and his worshipers must worship in spirit and in truth" (John 4:24). The reason your spirit man is not stronger than he is, is because you're feeding the flesh and starving the spirit. You're feeding the flesh all kinds of conversation, all kinds of relationships, all kinds of literature, all kinds of television shows. Sometimes you have to turn the television off, lay the magazine aside, take the phone off the hook, and get down on your knees and say, "Lord, I need more of your Spirit. Lord, I need more of your presence. I'm hungry, and I'm thirsty for you! Fill me with your power." "You will receive power when the Holy Spirit comes on you" (Acts 1:8). You need the power of God to do the will of

God, power to walk in his way, power to obey his voice, power to go higher and higher.

There are too many believers, too many children of God who are trying to live the life of God without the power of God. Without God's power, it's an impossible job, and you will surely fail. But when you get in Christ and are filled with the power of the Lord, you can sing, "I've got power that you can't see. God is living inside of me. I can fight any enemy, for God and me make a majority."

When the Lord comes into your life, he sets you free. He sets you free from the bondage of sin. You are legally free. You are judicially free. You have the victory. You have won the battle. But though you are legally and judicially free, the devil hangs around for a while. He won't give up. He tries to have some strongholds and some areas of influence in your life. You have to drive him out.

This is why the Bible says: "The weapons we fight with are not the weapons of the world. On the contrary, they have divine power to demolish strongholds" (2 Cor. 10:4).

We have spiritual weapons that are mighty through God. So we know for certain this fact: "You, dear children, are from God and have overcome them, because the one who is in you is greater than the one who is in the world" (1 John 4:4). Amen and amen!

notes

Chapter 1: Great Expectations

1. H. Cloud and J. Townsend, *Boundaries: When to Say Yes, When to Say No to Take Control of Your Life* (Grand Rapids: Zondervan 1992).
2. R. Stodghill II, "When Sex Is Kid Stuff," *Time*, June 15, 1998, 57.
3. Centers for Disease Control, "Tracking the Hidden Epidemics: Trends in STDs in the United States," 2001. www.cdc.gov.
4. S. L. Hader, D. K. Smith, J. S. Moore et al. "HIV Infection in Women in the United States—Status at the Millennium," *Journal of the American Medical Association* 285 (2001): 1186-91.
5. W. B. Russell, *Cracking Old Testament Codes: Literary Forms in the Hands of Preachers and Teachers* (Nashville: Broadman & Holman, 1995).
6. J. W. Hayford, "Why Sex Sins Are Worse Than Others," The King's College and Seminary, Van Nuys, CA. Soundword Tape #SC179 © Living Way Ministries.

Chapter 2: The Privilege of Parenting

1. "Kingdom Dynamics," *Spirit-Filled Life Bible (Nashville: Thomas Nelson*, 1991), 866.
2. T. M. Edwards, "Why Marry When You Can Stay Single?" *Time*, August 28, 2000, 46-55.
3. See *www.youthdevelopment.org*.
4. J. Dobson, *Complete Marriage and Family Home Reference Guide* (Wheaton, IL: Tyndale, 2000).

5. C. H. Hart, "Parents Do Matter: Combating the Myth That Parents Don't Matter," *Marriage and Families*, August 2000, 2-8.

6. Ibid., 3.

7. A. J. Hawkins, "Book Reviews: 1 Divorce Book, 2 Marriage Books." *Marriage and Families*, April 2001, 26-29.

Chapter 3: Raising God-Fearers

1. F. K. C. Price, *Higher Finance*. Order ID: 7PB46, Ever Increasing Faith Ministries, P.O. Box 90,000, Los Angeles, CA 90009. See *www.faithdome.org.*

Chapter 5: At Every Stage

1. W. R. Yount, *Created to Learn* (Nashville: Broadman & Holman, 1996), 49.

Chapter 7: What They're Learning in Sex Ed

1. L. Powlis, *The Black Women's Beauty Book* (New York: Doubleday, 1979).

2. G. Grant, *Grand Illusions: The Legacy of Planned Parenthood* (Brentwood, TN: Wolgemuth and Hyatt, Publishers, 1988).

3. J. Shaver, *Gianna: Aborted . . . and Lived to Tell About It* (Wheaton, IL: Tyndale House Publishers, 1998), 104-5.

4. M. Sanger, *Margaret Sanger: An Autobiography* (New York: W. W. Norton, 1938).

5. Ibid., 75.

6. Ibid., 375.

7. According to Sanger, "To each group we explained simply what contraception was; that abortion was the wrong way—no matter how early it was performed it was taking a life; that contraception was the better way, the safer way—it took a little time, a little trouble, but was well worth while in the long run, because life had not yet begun." Ibid., 217.

8. M. Sanger, *Women and the New Race* (New York: Brentanoís, 1920), 29.

9. Grant, *Grand Illusions*, p. 93.

10. Letter from Margaret Sanger to Dr. C. J. Gamble (December 10, 1939).

11. Letter from Margaret Sanger to D. Rose (March 8, 1941).

12. "What the Kaiser Family Foundation Is Not Saying About Sex Education in America: A Closer Look at the Kaiser Family Foundation Report, 'Sex Education in America: A View from Inside the Nation's Classrooms,'" *Focus on the Family*, October 5, 2000, 2.

13. J. Hayden, "The Condom Race," *Journal of American College Health* 42 (1993): 133-36.

Chapter 8: Clinics in the Schools

1. R. D. Glasow, Ph.D., *School-Based Clinics, The Abortion Connection* (Washington, DC: National Right to Life News, 1988).

2. J. Portner, "Clinton Health Plan Calls for Expanding School Clinic's Role," *Education Week, September 22, 1993, 1, 27; P. Schlafly, "Clinics Poised for Health Care Take," Washington Times, December 18, 1993, D3.*

3. J. G. Dryfoos, "School-Based Social and Health Services for At-Risk Students," *Urban Education* 26 (1991): 118-37.

4. "The Comprehensive School-Health Education Workshop," *Journal of School Health [Special issue], January 1993, 63.*

5. M. Sanger, *Pivot of Civilization* (New York: Brentano, 1992), and *Margaret Sanger: An Autobiography (New York: W. W. Norton, 1938).*

6. C. Valenza, "Was Margaret Sanger a Racist?" *Family Planning Perspectives* 17 (1985): 44-46.

7. R. Farley, *Growth of the Black Population* (Chicago: Markham, 1970).

8. F. L. Gobble, C. E. Vincent, C. M. Cochrane, and F. R. Lock, "A Nonmedical Approach to Fertility Reduction," *Obstetrics and Gynecology* 34 (1969): 888-91; S. C. Scheyer, "DHEW's New Center: The National Commitment to Family Planning," *Family Life Educator* 14, no. 2 (1970), 4-10.

9. L. M. Hellman, "Five-Year Plan for Population Research and Family Planning Services," *Family Planning Perspectives* 3 (1971): 35-40.

10. A. F. Guttmacher and H. Pilpel, "Abortion and the Unwanted Child," *Family Planning Perspectives* 2 (1970): 16-24.

11. Planned Parenthood of New York City, "Family Planning in New York City: Recommendations for Action," *Family Planning Perspectives* 2 (1970): 25-31.

12. D. Kirby, "School-Based Clinics Enter the 90s: Update Evaluation and Future Challenges" [report] (1989). Washington, DC: Center for Population Options [Advocates for Youth]. (ERIC Document Reproduction Service No. ED 320 209.)

13. P. M. Sarrel and L. J. Sarrel, "Birth-Control Services and Sex Counseling at Yale," *Family Planning Perspectives* 3 (1971): 33-36.

14. H. F. Pilpel and N. F. Wechsler, "Birth-Control, Teen-agers and the Law: A New Look," *Family Planning Perspectives* 3 (1971): 37-45.

15. *Population and the American Future* (New York: Signet, 1972), 183-90.

16. Ibid.

17. Ibid., 154.

18. Ibid., 170.

19. P. D. Harvey, "Condoms—A New Look," *Family Planning Perspectives* 4 (1972): 27-30.

20. D. S. F. Settlage, S. Baroff, and D. Cooper, "Sexual Experience of Younger Teenage Girls Seeking Contraceptive Assistance for the First Time," *Family Planning Perspectives* 5 (1973): 223-26.

21. L. E. Edwards, M. E. Steinman, K. A. Arnold, and E. Y. Hakanson, "Adolescent Pregnancy Prevention Services in High School Clinics," *Family Planning Perspectives* 12 (1980): 6-14.

22. J. Dryfoos, "School-Based Health Clinics: A New Approach to Preventing Adolescent Pregnancy?" *Family Planning Perspectives* 17 (1985): 70-75.

23. Ibid.

24. K. L. Feroli, S. K. Hobson, E. S. Miola, P. N. Scott, and G. D. Waterfield, "School-Based Clinics: The Baltimore Experience," *Journal of Pediatric Health Care* 6 (1992): 127-31.

25. Dryfoos, "School-Based Health Clinics," 70-75.

26. E. W. Paul and H. F. Pilpel, "Teenagers and Pregnancy: The Law in 1979," *Family Planning Perspectives* 11 (1979): 297-301.

27. J. Kasun, "Sex Education: A New Philosophy for America?" *The Family in America*, July 1989, 8.

28. C. Warren, *Improving Students' Access to Health Care: School-Based Health Clinics: A Briefing Paper for Policy Makers* (New York: Center for Public Advocacy Research, Ford Foundation, 1987) (ERIC Document Reproduction Service No. ED 295 072); "School-Based Clinics That Work" [report] (Rockville, MD: Public Health Services, U.S. Department of Health and Human Services, June 1993) (ERIC Document Reproduction Service No. ED 359 189).

29. J. Kozol, *Savage Inequities: Children in America's Schools* (New York: HarperCollins, 1991).

30. "The Comprehensive School-Health Education Workshop," *Journal of School Health* [Special issue], January 1993, 63.

31. See *www.advocatesforyouth.org*.

32. J. G. Dryfoos, "School-Based Health Clinics: Three Years of Experience," *Family Planning Perspectives* 20 (1988): 193-200.

33. J. D. Forrest and S. Singh, "The Sexual and Reproductive Behavior of American Women, 1982-1988," *Family Planning Perspectives* 22 (1990): 206-14; "Premarital Sexual Experience Among Adolescent Women—United States, 1970-1988," *Morbidity and Mortality Weekly Report* 39 (1991): 929-32.

34. C. D. Brindis, "Evaluating School-Based Clinic Programs," *Clinic News* 4, no. 2 (1988), 3-8.

35. D. de Mauro, "Sexuality Education 1990: A Review of State Sexuality and AIDS Education Curricula," *SIECUS Report* 18 (1989/1990): 1-9.

36. S. E. Weed, J. DeGaston, J. Prigmore, and R. Tanas, "The Teen-Aid Family Life Education Project: Fourth Year Evaluation Report Prepared for the Office of

Adolescent Pregnancy Programs (OAPP)" (Salt Lake City: Institute for Research and Evaluation, 1991).

37. L. J. Kolbe, L. Kann, J. L. Collins, M. L. Small, B. C. Pateman, and C. W. Warren, "The School-Health Policies and Programs Study (SHPPS): Context, Methods, General Findings, and Future Efforts," *Journal of School Health* 65 (1995): 339-43; D. H. McKinney and G. L. Peak, *School-Based and School-Linked Health Centers: Update 1994* (Washington, DC: Advocates for Youth [Center for Population Options], 1994).

38. L. Tolbert, "Teaching Abstinence: Legislators Just Said No," *Los Angeles Times* (June 6, 1998): B7.

39. M. Ebert, "Will Condoms Land Schools in Court? *Focus on the Family Citizen* 8 (1994): 10-11.

Chapter 9: Condoms—Just in Case?

1. P. Donovan, "Testing Positive: Sexually Transmitted Disease and the Public Health Response" [report] (New York: The Alan Guttmacher Institute, 1993).

2. "Sexual Behavior Among High School Students—United States 1990," *Morbidity and Mortality Weekly Report* 40 (1992): 885-88.

3. J. Santelli, M. Alexander, M. Farmer, T. Johnson, B. Rosenthal, and D. Hotra, "Bringing Parents into School Clinics: Parent Attitudes Toward School Clinics and Contraception," *Journal of Adolescent Health* 13 (1992): 269-74; B. Wright and K. Cranston, "Condom Availability in a Small Town: Lessons from Falmouth, Massachusetts," *SIECUS Report* 21 (October/November 1992): 13-17.

4. D. A. Dawson, "The Effects of Sex Education on Adolescent Behavior," *Family Planning Perspectives* 18 (1986): 162-70; W. Marsiglio and F. L. Mott, "The Impact of Sex Education on Sexual Activity, Contraceptive Use and Premarital Pregnancy Among American Teenagers," *Family Planning Perspectives* 18 (1986): 151-62.

5. J. A. Olsen and S. E. Weed, "Effects of Family-Planning Programs for Teenagers on Adolescent Birth and Pregnancy Rates," *Family Planning Perspectives* 20 (1987): 153-95.

6. R. L. Armacost, "Comments on 'Six School-Based Clinics: Their Reproductive Health Services and Impact on Sexual Behavior'" (unpublished manuscript, University of Central Florida, 1991).

7. J. A. Seybert, "Health Habits of Urban High School Students: Evaluation of School-Based Clinics" (paper presented at the annual meeting of theAmerican Educational Research Association, New Orleans, April 1988).

8. J. O. G. Billy, K. L. Brewster, and W. R. Grady, "Contextual Effects on the Sexual Behavior of Adolescent Women," *Journal of Marriage and the Family* 56 (1994): 400.

9. P. R. Newman, "The Peer Group," in B. B. Wolman, ed., *Handbook of Developmental Psychology* (Englewood Cliffs, NJ: Prentice-Hall, 1982), 535.

10. G. C. Griffin, "Condoms and Contraceptives in Junior High and High School Clinics: What Do You Think?" *Postgraduate Medicine* 93, no. 5 (1993), 1-6.

11. Fehlauer, E., "Attitudes, Influences, and Expectations of Adolescent Dating Behaviors: A Study of High School Students," *Masters Abstracts International* (University of Alberta, 1992), 1444.

12. Billy et al., "Contextual Effects on the Sexual Behavior of Adolescent Women," 387-404.

13. C. Brindis, S. Starbuck-Morales, A. L. Wolfe, and V. McCarter, "Characteristics Associated with Contraceptive Use Among Adolescent Females in School-Based Family Planning Programs," *Family Planning Perspectives* 26 (1994): 160-64.

14. Ibid.

15. D. Kirby, "Six School-Based Clinics: Their Reproductive Health Services and Impact on Sexual Behavior," *Family Planning Perspectives* 23 (1991): 6-16; K. J. Pittman, P. M. Wilson, S. Adams-Taylor, and S. Randolph, "Making Sexuality Education and Prevention Programs Relevant for African-American Youth," *Journal of School Health* 62, no. 7 (1992): 339-44.

16. S. E. Weed, J. DeGaston, J. Prigmore, and R. Tanas, "The Teen-Aid Family Life Education Project" (Fourth Year Evaluation Report Prepared for the Office of Adolescent Pregnancy Programs, Institute for Research and Evaluation, Salt Lake City, 1991).

17. R. M. Lerner and J. A. Shea, "Social Behavior in Adolescence," in B. B. Wolman, ed., *Handbook of Developmental Psychology* (Englewood Cliffs, NJ: Prentice-Hall, 1982), 503-25.

18. L. C. Ku, F. L. Sonenstein, and J. H. Pleck, "The Association of AIDS Education and Sex Education with Sexual Behavior and Condom Use Among Teenage Men," *Family Planning Perspectives* 24 (1995): 100-106; S. E. Weed, J. A. Olsen, J. DeGaston, and J. Prigmore, "Predicting and Changing Teen Sexual Activity Rates: A Comparison of Three Title XX Programs" (Salt Lake City: Institute for Research and Evaluation, 1992).

19. R. H. DuRant, C. S. Ashworth, C. Newman, and G. Gaillard, "High School Students' Knowledge of HIV/AIDS and Perceived Risk of Currently Having AIDS," *Journal of School Health* 62 (1992): 59-63; B. C. Hodges, M. Leavy, R. Swift, and R. S. Gold, "Gender and Ethnic Differences in Adolescents' Attitudes Toward Condom Use," *Journal of School Health* 62 (1992): 103-6; J. Trussell, D. L. Warner, and R. A. Hatcher, "Condom Slippage and Breakage Rates," *Family Planning Perspectives* 24 (1992): 20-23.

20. "What the Kaiser Family Foundation Is Not Saying About Sex Education in America: A Closer Look at the Kaiser Family Foundation Report: 'Sex Education in America: A View from Inside the Nation's Classrooms'" *Focus on*

the Family, October 5, 2000; B. Stackhouse, "The Impact of Religion on Sexuality Education," *SIECUS Report* 18 (1989/90): 21-27.

21. "Future Directions: HIV/AIDS Education in the Nation's Schools" (New York: Sex Information and Education Council of the United States, 1992).

22. "Take Twelve: The Truth Behind 12 of the Most Common Arguments Made by Powerful 'Safe-Sex' Organizations Against the Abstinence-Until-Marriage Message," *Focus on the Family*, (2001).

23. Best Friends Foundation, "Best Friends Participation in Title V Abstinence Education Evaluation" (February 10, 2000), 4455 Connecticut Ave., NW, Suite 310, Washington, DC 20008.

24. See the A. C. Green Youth Foundation, I've Got the Power Abstinence Curriculum, at www.acgreen.com or 1-800-AC-YOUTH.

25. See Project Reality, The Game Plan, at www.projectreality.org or 1-847-729-3298.

26. See National Clearinghouse for Abstinence Education at www.abstinence.net.

27. See *www.family.org*.

28. See Christian Educators Association International at *www.ceai.org*.

29. See Character Education Partnership at www.cep.org.

Chapter 10: Children at Risk

1. P. B. Johnson, and H. L. Johnson, "Reaffirming the Power of Parental Influence on Adolescent Smoking and Drinking Decisions," *Adolescent and Family Health* 2, no. 1 (Spring 2001), 37-43.

2. Ibid., 37.

3. Ibid., 39.

4. Ibid.

5. Ibid., 43.

6. L. McLaughlin, "In Brief," *Time*, December 18, 2000.

Chapter 11: God's Standard Is Abstinence

1. L. S. Kastner, "Ecological Factors Predicting Adolescent Contraceptive Use: Implications for Intervention," *Journal of Adolescent Health Care* 5 (1984): 79-86; D. A. Dawson, "The Effects of Sex Education on Adolescent Behavior," *Family Planning Perspectives* 18 (1986): 162-70; P. L. Benson and M. J. Donahue, "Ten-Year Trends in At-Risk Behaviors: A National Study of Black Adolescents," *Journal of Adolescent Research* 4 (1989): 125-39; B. C. Miller and K. A. Moore, "Adolescent Sexual Behavior, Pregnancy, and Parenting: Research Through the 1980s," *Journal of Marriage and the Family* 52 (1990): 1029-30; S. Parker, *Special Report: Sex and Our Youth* (Anaheim, CA: Traditional Values Coalitions Action Alert, 1994); L. Tolbert, "Condom Availability Through School-Based Clinics

and Teenagers' Attitudes Regarding Premarital Sexual Activity" (doctoral diss., Talbot School of Theology, 1996).

2. *60 Minutes*, Sunday, June 24, 2001.

3. Centers for Disease Control, "Condoms for Prevention of Sexually Transmitted Diseases," *Public Health Reports* 16 (1988): 13-20.

4. "10,000 Physicians to Ask for Resignation of CDC Director, End of Cover-Up," (23 July 2001). Press release. The Physicians Consortium. 1240 N Mountain Rd, Harrisburg, PA 17112.

5. See *www.balmingilead.org.*

6. *Healing Begins Here: A Pastor's Guidebook for HIV/AIDS Ministry Through the Church* (California Department of Health Services Office of AIDS, June 2000), 95.

7. Ibid.

8. Ibid., 23-25.

9. Ibid., 25.

10. Ibid., introduction to Sermon Notes.

11. "Ten Churches Observe AIDS Awareness Sunday," *Los Angeles Sentinel* (October 10, 1991), C11.

12. "For the Record," *Los Angeles Times* (October 19, 1991), B3.

13. "Word Wealth," *Spirit-Filled Life Bible* (Nashville: Thomas Nelson, 1991), 1710.

14. J. S. Feinberg and P. D. Feinberg, *Ethics for a Brave New World* (Wheaton, IL: Crossway, 1993), 177.

15. Ibid.

16. Focus on the Family, Declaration on Sexual Morality (www.family.org).

17. The Physicians Consortium, "A Perspective on the Medical Implications of the Virginity Pledge Among Teens" [report] (January 5, 2001), 1240 North Mountain Rd., Harrisburg, PA 17112.

18. Ibid.

19. Ibid., 3.

20. Ibid., 7.

21. Ibid., 3.

22. Ibid.

23. Ibid.

24. P. Fagan, "Sex, Religion and Parents: Teen Pregnancy and the Facts of Life" *The Heritage Foundation* (unpublished paper), 11.

25. Ibid., 8.

Chapter 12: Healing, Hope, Power

1. See *www.family.org.*

2. For curriculum on teacher training, see *www.teachinglikejesus.org.*

3. See *www.ceai.org.*

4. American Center for Law and Justice, *www.aclj.org.*

5. See *www.aclj.org/publications/kyr/app—1.asp.*

6. American Center for Law and Justice in Virginia, P.O. Box 64429, Virginia Beach, VA 23467. Phone 757-226-2489.

7. Mark Senter III, *The Coming Revolution in Youth Ministry* (Wheaton, IL: Victor, 1992).

8. California Released-Time Christian Education Association, Inc., 1534 N. Amador Ave., Ontario, CA 91764-1402. Phone 909-982-8300.

9. See *www.bringinghopetoyouth.org.*

10. See *www.biblecurriculum.org.*

11. C. Colson, "Reversing Memory Loss," *Christianity Today* 45, no. 10 (2001), 88.

12. See *www.bringinghopetoyouth.org.*

13. For more information on how to care for public schools, visit *www.Iamforschools. com* and *www.ceai.org.*

14. See *info@youthworkers.net* and *www.gospelcom.net/yfc/.*

15. See *ys@youthspecialties.com.*

16. See *www.uywi.org.*

17. See *www.faithdome.org.*

18. For more information, check the yellow pages under Abortion Alternatives or call Focus on the Family's Crisis Pregnancy Ministry at 719-531-3460.

19. See *www.churchrisk.com.*

20. N. Hare and J. Hare, *Bringing the Black Boy to Manhood* (San Francisco: Black Think Tank, 1985).

Appendix A: Declaration on Sexual Morality

1. Lev. 11:44-45; 19:2; 20:7, 26: 1 Peter 1:16.

2. Rom. 8:5-8; 13:14; 1 Cor. 2:14; 1 Thess. 4:3-5; 2 Tim. 2:22; James 1:14; 1John 2:15-16; Jude 19.

3. Lev. 20:7-21, 26; 1 Cor. 6:18-20; Eph. 1:4; 5:3; 1 Thess. 4:3-7; Heb. 13:4; 1Peter 1:15-16.

4. Job 31:1; Matt. 5:28; Phil. 4:8; James 1:14-15.

5. 1 Thess. 4:6.

6. Lev. 18:7-10; 19:29; 2 Sam. 13:1-22; Prov. 6:26; 23:27; Matt. 5:28; 1 Thess. 4:3-7; 1 Peter 4:3; 2 Peter 2:13-14.

7. Prov. 5:18-19; 6:32-33; John 15:10-11.

8. 1 Cor. 7:36-38.

9. Gen. 2:24; Mal. 2:14-15; Matt. 19:4-6; Mark 10:6-8; 1 Cor. 7:39; Rom. 7:2; Eph. 5:31.

10. Mal. 2:14-15; Matt. 19:6; Mark 10:9.

11. Deut. 24:1-4; Matt. 19:9; 1 Cor. 7:15.

12. Eph. 5:30-33; 1 Cor. 6:12-20.

13. 1 Cor. 7:3-5.

14. Exod. 20:14; Lev. 18:7-17, 20; Deut. 5:18; Matt. 19:9, 18; Mark 10:19; Luke 18:20; Rom. 13:9; 1 Cor. 6:13, 18; Gal. 5:19; Eph. 5:3; 1 Thess. 4:3; Heb. 13:4.

15. Matt. 5:27-28; 2 Tim. 2:22.

16. Rom. 1:24; 1 Thess. 4:8.

17. Prov. 5:3-14.

18. Rom. 1:32; 1 Cor. 6:9-10; Eph. 5:3-5; Jude 13; Rev. 22:15.

19. Lev. 18:22; 20:13; Rom. 1:26-27; 1 Cor. 6:9; 1 Tim. 1:10.

20. Gen. 2:24; Rom. 1:24-25.

21. 1 Cor. 6:9-11; 1 John 1:9.

22. Gal. 6:7.

23. Rom. 12:15; Luke 19:10.

24. John 8:11.

Appendix B: Shall We Go on Sinning?

1. Bishop Charles E. Blake, pastor of West Angeles Church of God in Christ, Los Angeles, CA, Sunday, July 8, 2001, 11:00 A.M. Edited message from Tape # CEB-070801.

CPSIA information can be obtained at www.ICGtesting.com
Printed in the USA
BVOW041635240113

311500BV00001B/40/P